To

Happy

Birthday!,

♡ Aunt

Shari

Secrets of the Signs

STACEY WOLF

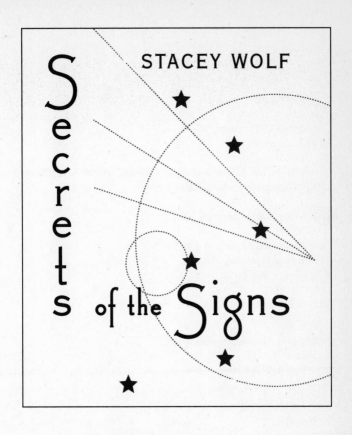

Secrets of the Signs

WARNER BOOKS

A Time Warner Company

Warner Books, Inc., 1271 Avenue of the Americas, New York, NY 10020
Visit our Web site at www.twbookmark.com

 A Time Warner Company

Printed in the United States of America
First Printing: September 2000
10 9 8 7 6 5 4 3 2 1

Library of Congress Cataloging-in-Publication Data

Wolf, Stacey.
    Secrets of the signs / by Stacey Wolf.
        p. cm.
        ISBN 0-446-67719-1
        1. Astrology. I. Title.

    BF1708.1.W65 2000
    133.5—dc21
                                            00-039899

Book design and text composition by L&G McRee
Cover design by Rachel McClain

CONTENTS

CONTENTS

See how you get along with every sign in the zodiac.
Each relationship comparison has a star rating system
to help you figure out how compatible you are with romantic partners, friends, and parents.

After you graduate from Sun signs, get deeper into astrology. Check out *Moon Signs* (the inside you),
Venus Signs (you in love), and *Mars Signs* (you at
play) for a broader profile of your personality and the
compatibility of your relationships.

Venus, Mars, and Moon charts describe your total personality as well as your compatibility with friends and
sweethearts.

INTRODUCTION

Look around. The world is changing. More earth-quakes and hurricanes. Compromise and peace where we never thought the fighting would end. It's no coincidence that this is all happening now. As we move deeper into the new millennium, we move deeper into the Age of Aquarius.

For the past 2,000 years, we've rumbled through the Piscean Age, which gave us organized religion, holy wars, and the industrial age. Ugh. The Aquarian Age will bring us "harmony and understanding, sympathy and trust abounding." Okay, that's from a song from the first whiff of this flower-power age, but it's really true. There will be more global unity. We will reach out a hand to help others. More people will discover their individuality, start their own companies, and live by their soul. The Internet and the stockholding millionaire next door are products of the Aquarian Age.

You are the first generation to come of age in Aquarius. In astrological terms you are very special and unique. You were born with an innate understanding of the world. You care about what happens to people and know you can make a difference. Because of this, astrology is second nature to you—you just might not know it yet.

Secrets of the Signs is your key, your handbook to the future. This book will help you learn about yourself, your motivations, and the way you operate in the world. You will find out about your Sun sign and the other vital aspects of your astrological makeup: your Moon sign and the placement of Venus and Mars in your chart.

Astrology enables us to better understand the dynamics of our interactions, it leads us to discover the deeper meaning within our relationships, and it helps us find the love we are meant to have. *Secrets of the Signs* will be your guide in picking supportive friends, finding that perfect sweetheart, and getting along with your parents. And it will help you to avoid potentially negative relationships, to get what you want more often—and to have more fun in the process. By the time you finish turning these pages, you will be able to figure out your

Introduction

compatibility with anyone you know—friends, teachers, siblings, even celebrities!

What does your Sun sign tell you about yourself? What sign is your Venus? Where was the Moon at the time of your birth? Check out the stars!

CHAPTER 1

Astrology 101

A REALLY BRIEF HISTORY

People have been calculating the movements of the Sun and the Moon for at least 7,000 years. The ancient Hindus divided the heavens into 28 equal parts, representing the 28-day cycle of the Moon. The ancient Chinese also divided the sky into 28 equal parts they called Mansions of the Moon. Western astrology is based on a different principle, calculating the movements of the Sun.

The foundation of today's system can be found in ancient Babylon. About 4000 B.C., the Sumerians began recording the cycles of the Sun, the Moon, and the harvest. As their culture got more sophisticated, they built observation towers called ziggurats. From 300 feet up, they observed the movements of the Sun, Venus, and Mars. As new planets were discovered, they were given specific characteristics and a mythical god to rule over them. The heavens were divided into twelve sections, each governing a specific influence of daily life. Many of these sections, or houses, still keep the same names today.

For much of our recent past, we were only aware of the Sun and six celestial moving bodies: the Moon, Mercury, Mars, Venus, Jupiter, and Saturn. Modern astrology began with the discovery of three new planets: Uranus in 1781, Neptune in 1846, and Pluto in 1930. With each new discovery, we enter into a new astrological understanding. Each planet has its own set of characteristics that influence our lives. As each planet was discovered, astrologers determined its accurate place in the astrological world and assigned it to rule over specific houses and signs. The twelve astrological houses and their corresponding signs share ruling planets, since there aren't enough to go around.

TWELVE HOUSES, TWELVE SIGNS

The key to mastering astrology is understanding the twelve houses and the twelve signs. To understand the way the ancient Babylonians divided the sky into twelve houses, think of the solar system as a big pizza cut into twelve slices. The Earth is in the center of the pie—not because it is the center of the universe, but because we live on it! Each of the houses, or slices of the pie, represents another aspect of life: our personality, our home life, our careers, our creativity, and so on.

Each of the twelve slices of the pie has a different topping—and you enjoy them all for different reasons. Those are the twelve signs (see chart on p. 4). Each of the twelve signs has different characteristics—good and bad—but no one is more or less interesting or fulfilling than another.

The houses are named after the constellations in each of them, and in turn, those constellations are the names of the twelve signs of the zodiac: Aries, Taurus, Gemini, Cancer, Leo, Virgo, Libra, Scorpio, Sagittarius, Capricorn, Aquarius, and Pisces. The sign of Aries rules the first house, Taurus rules the second, and so on. The next time you're at a party and someone asks you, "What's your sign?" you'll know that it literally is the place in the stars where the Sun was at the time of your birth.

Because each sign is at home in a specific house, the descriptions of the twelve different areas of our lives correspond to the basic Sun sign personalities. For example, the first house corresponds to Aries; it rules

SECRETS OF THE SIGNS

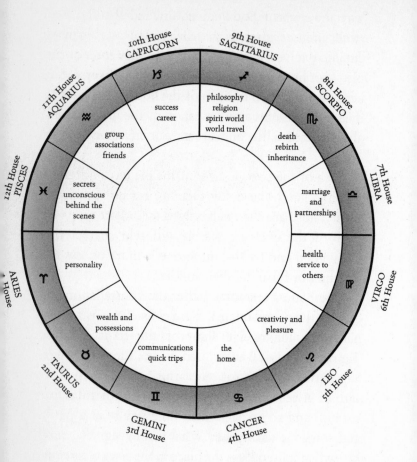

10th House CAPRICORN — success career

9th House SAGITTARIUS — philosophy religion spirit world world travel

11th House AQUARIUS — group associations friends

8th House SCORPIO — death rebirth inheritance

12th House PISCES — secrets unconscious behind the scenes

7th House LIBRA — marriage and partnerships

ARIES ... House — personality

VIRGO 6th House — health service to others

TAURUS 2nd House — wealth and possessions

LEO 5th House — creativity and pleasure

GEMINI 3rd House — communications quick trips

CANCER 4th House — the home

over the personality. People born under the sign of Aries are energetic, headstrong people. The second house, the house of money and possessions, corresponds to the second sign, Taurus. Taureans like to collect nice things and are possessive about them. The third house is the communications house, corresponding to Gemini, the zodiac's great communicator. All the houses and their Sun signs are related this way.

THE INFLUENCE OF THE NINE PLANETS

Okay, you all know that the Sun isn't the only body that moves around in the sky above us. In Western astrology the Sun is the single most important factor in determining your personality, but it is not the only one. The Moon along with the other planets in the solar system (Mercury, Venus, Mars, Jupiter, Saturn, Uranus, Neptune, and Pluto) also affect your daily life. (You don't really count Earth because you're on it.)

Each planet's place in the universe influences us in its own unique way, and because they move around at different speeds—this is where it gets complicated—they end up in different houses and different signs at different times. Depending upon where they show up in your chart, and how strong your Sun sign is, they will influence your personality and your future in various ways.

Although a professional horoscope includes all of these aspects of astrology—the twelve houses, the twelve signs, the Sun, the Moon, and the eight planets—this book is focused on the signs of your Sun, Moon, Venus, and Mars. The Moon's position, the second most important factor in our personal astrology makeup, tells you about your emotions and your unconscious. The planet Venus shows what you're like in the love category, and Mars shows your personality at play. Together, the relationship between Mars and Venus reveals a lot about the kinds of love we attract and the perfect partners for us. There's more about that in chapter 5, "Beyond the Basics."

The Four Elements

Before you are let loose in the Sun sign section, you need to know one more thing about basic astrology. The twelve signs are divided into a few subgroups. The most important of these is the group of four natural elements. The members of these four groups have similar personality traits even though they have different signs.

The four elements of nature are: fire, earth, air, and water. Each element has three signs in its group:

Fire: Aries, Leo, Sagittarius
Earth: Taurus, Capricorn, Virgo
Air: Gemini, Libra, Aquarius
Water: Cancer, Scorpio, Pisces

Your element will give you a good idea of your personality even before you read about your own Sun sign.

Fire: Natural leaders, aggressive, fearless
Earth: Methodical, tender, practical
Air: Intelligent, quick thinking, social
Water: Intuitive, compassionate, emotional

If you know someone else's element, you can get a basic idea of whether you are going to get along with them.

Fire + Fire: Fire and fire make more fire. Whoa! This can get out of control!

Fire + Earth: Fire scorches earth. Fire signs are too dominant, and earth signs are too determined. Not a great match.

Fire + Air: Air fans the fire. This combination is supportive to the core.

Fire + Water: Water puts out fire. Fire signs lose their power when they bend to watery sensitivities.

Earth + Earth: Earth and earth: Mmmm—more dirt! Earth signs understand each other and dig each other, but their similarity can be a turnoff.

Earth + Air: Earth and air, both just there. If you think about it, the land and atmosphere don't really do much for each other; the same is true in astrology.

Earth + Water: Water makes earth grow. Water signs' intuition brings out the best in earth signs.

Air + Air: More air to breathe! Social air signs can't get enough of each other.

Air + Water: Water and air just sit there—another two elements that have very little to do with each other.

Water + Water: More to drink, more to drown in. Two water signs together can bring out the best and the worst in each other—to the extreme.

Now that you've got the basics—the planets, houses, signs, and elements—you can move on to the different Sun signs and find out what makes them unique.

CHAPTER 2

You Are Who You Are: Understanding Your Sun Sign

The Sun sign is the most important astrological aspect. The placement of the Sun at the time of your birth determines your personality and your operating style. This chapter describes each sign, beginning with the traditional first sign, Aries, and moving through to the last sign, Pisces.

The dates listed for the Sun signs vary slightly year to year. These dates are the most accurate, but since we constructed our clocks around the movements of the Sun and not vice versa, the exact moment the Sun moves from one sign into another varies slightly every year. For example, you may be both born on March 20th *and* an Aries—occasionally that happens.

If you are born within a day or two of the dates listed, you are born on the cusp of two signs. That means your main influence is the sign you are born under, but you can expect to be highly influenced by the sign standing next to your own. Read the descriptions of both signs to see how they influence you in different ways.

To discover what makes you tick and find a focus for your future, read on!

| ARIES | FIRE | MARCH 21–APRIL 19 |

Ruling Planet: Mars
Lucky Day: Tuesday
Famous Aries: Warren Beatty, Lucy Lawless, Mariah Carey
Best Traits: You have a dynamic and energetic presence, tackling every experience with a bit of moxie.
Biggest Problems: You have a tendency to project your thoughts and desires on others, which can make you seem kind of selfish. Sometimes you just don't understand why people don't want the same things you do.

Trademark: "I'm a legend in my own mind."
Best Job: Athlete, environmental activist.
Worst Job: Buddhist monk.
What You Love: Rabble-rousing with a group of your best friends. You're definitely the loudest.
What You Hate: Taking orders. Playing Follow the Leader.
Best Way to Make a Million Bucks: Setting goals, then corralling others to complete the project.
Best Way to Spend a Million Bucks: Creating an elaborate stage production—starring yourself!
Your Secret Desire: To conquer the world.
Best Gifts to Give You: CDs that you can turn up real loud, so you can dance and sing your heart out!

Aries are fireballs. You're driven, passionate, and impulsive, fiercely loyal friends and active crusaders. Rams love to set goals and achieve them in your headstrong way. The only problem is that after you start a project your energy fizzles, and then you lose interest. Aries are great at rousing others into action, so let them finish your project for you!

You're bursting with energy, and because of that you speak without thinking. What you say can be a bit bruising and tactless, but you mean no harm. With all that energy it's sometimes hard to think first and speak second. Yes, you can have a short fuse at times, but your dynamic and talkative nature far outweighs any impulsiveness people may see.

You hate taking care of the small details of life and disdain domestic chores—you're just too important to be cleaning a bathroom, even if it's your own. You're much better at living in the moment than at seeing things through. Patience isn't one of the Rams' virtues. You can't imagine sitting through something you dislike for more than a minute.

You are independent to the max, fun-loving, and always open to a new experience. You're always in great demand. Whatever you want is yours, child of Aries. If you don't earn it, you'll get it by sheer force.

| TAURUS | EARTH | APRIL 20–MAY 20 |

Ruling Planet: Venus

Lucky Day: Friday

Famous Taureans: Cher, Jerry Seinfeld, Michelle Pfeiffer

Best Traits: You have a steady and relentless ambition, yet you're gentle and loving to the core. You create peace and stability wherever you go.

Biggest Problems: You're the most stubborn of all in the zodiac—and it takes a lot of stubbornness to win this prize. Your possessive streak gets you in trouble with romantic partners. It's okay to let them out of your sight!

Trademark: "I'm not obstinate. I just know what's best, that's all."

Best Job: Working with high-rolling bankers; stabilizing the risk brings you huge rewards.

Worst Job: Bus driver, speedboat captain.

What You Love: Long-lasting friendships and relationships.

What You Hate: People who are satisfied with less than perfection.

Best Way to Make a Million Bucks: The hard work, fun, and excitement of seeing your work efforts turn to gold.

Best Way to Spend a Million Bucks: Collecting property and possessions. You love owning nice things—the more the better.

Your Secret Desire: To hole up at home with the perfect mate, have a great meal, and snuggle by the fire till dawn.

Best Gifts to Give You: Expensive collectibles.

Those born under the sign of Taurus are detail-oriented and persistent, headstrong and artistic. Your need for stability often leads to a job in finance, but being ruled by Venus makes you a great designer and artist. With your keen eye for making money and your innate understanding of value, you are great at picking stocks, buying fine art, and accumulating wealth.

Bulls hate change—it goes against your methodical nature. You like to create permanence in your life—from your job to your friends to your relationship. You hesitate to go for something if you know it's not going to last. You love the safety and stability of routine, so moving on requires much contemplation before you will take action. A Bull won't be rushed.

You're happiest at home, surrounded by lots of grass and trees, expensive things, and your partner. Not the most gregarious of signs, Bulls socialize with the few friends you keep for many years.

You can be extremely generous, and you enjoy pleasing others. At your best you are independent, patient, dependable, and instinctive. At your worst you can also be intolerant, suspicious, and secretive—but thanks to your easygoing nature we don't see that side of you very often.

| GEMINI | AIR | MAY 21–JUNE 20 |

Ruling Planet: Mercury
Lucky Day: Wednesday
Famous Geminis: Paula Abdul, Donald Trump, Venus Williams
Best Traits: You're so clever, energetic, and funny that you can talk yourself out of any sticky situation.

Biggest Problems: You find it hard to focus on one thing at a time. You get bored quickly.

Trademark: "I just wanna have fun!"

Best Job: Stand-up comedian, gossip columnist.

Worst Job: Brain surgeon.

What You Love: Going to parties, setting fashion trends.

What You Hate: Finishing projects you've started.

Best Way to Make a Million Bucks: Selling anything to anyone at any time for any price.

Best Way to Spend a Million Bucks: Buying shoes, clothing, and accessories.

Your Secret Desire: To date two celebrities at once.

Best Gift to Give You: A cell phone.

Gemini, you're the great communicator of the zodiac. You're a natural writer and public speaker—and you don't need a special occasion to be chatty. You're intelligent and quick-witted, and your curiosity keeps you constantly doing new things, learning new skills. Knowing so much about so many different things makes you great fun at parties, but can make you appear a bit light and superficial. Which is, by the way, exactly the way you like it!

Ruled by the symbol of the Twins, you have a dual nature. You're good at juggling at least two things at once. Adaptable Gemini is willing to try anything. The problem is that you end up doing *every-thing,* scattering your energy and accomplishing less than you'd like. You may dread focusing on one task at a time, but the key to your success is to find the perfect pace for yourself—that way you'll get to do everything you want. Better to be a little bored than to be left without anything to show for your efforts.

You're a bundle of energy, and so much fun to be around that you have tons of friends and can win many favors from high places. Fickle with food, you like to eat little meals throughout the day rather than eating three big meals at prearranged times. You have a fabulous flair for fad and fashion, and you instinctively know what's hot before everyone else does—and then you coolly drop it for the next new trend, wearing everything with style and grace.

Gemini, you thrive on change, live life in the moment, and love to find shortcuts. Best of all, you're well aware of your strengths, and use them to your advantage. Whatever you want to do, go for it, Gemini.

| CANCER | WATER | JUNE 21–JULY 22 |

Ruling Planet: The Moon
Lucky Day: Monday

Famous Cancers: Tom Cruise; Courtney Love; Diana, Princess of Wales

Best Traits: Your sympathetic and intuitive nature touches everyone you meet. You're at your best creating a loving home and family environment.

Biggest Problems: You can sulk and brood for days when you feel slighted. Sometimes you can be too sensitive and insecure for your own good.

Trademark: "I feel your pain."

Best Job: Psychologist, author.

Worst Job: Race car driver, fighter pilot.

What You Love: Keeping in touch with classmates, friends, and sweethearts from the past—others would've dropped these people long ago.

What You Hate: Flamboyant, shallow, self-righteous people.

Best Way to Make a Million Bucks: Understanding the thoughts and feelings of others.

Best Way to Spend a Million Bucks: Buying gifts for down-and-out friends.

Your Secret Desire: To stay close to home, helping every stray dog, cat, and human you meet in the neighborhood.

Best Gifts to Give You: Beautiful plush pillows for your house, a soft sensual bathrobe for yourself.

Cancers are sensitive and intuitive, but also insecure and withdrawn. Due to the Moon's influence, your moods and emotions flow like the tide. You're happy one day, gloomy the next. Everything happens under the surface with the Crab, far below the defenses of your tough shell. Some signs like to tell it like it is. With Cancers it's what you're *not* saying that's important. People who know you need some intuition of their own to understand what's happening with you on the inside.

You're a sympathetic listener, and people—from friends to clients, co-workers to strangers—flock to you with their problems. Cancers exude intuitive understanding from the depths of their soul. Caught on a bad day, though, you can be restless, indifferent, and filled with self-pity.

You are a romantic and dreamy partner who loves to create a safe living environment. You are the universe's nurturer. Nothing is better than showering your mate with love and affection. All that attention is wonderful, but your mate may find it stifling at times.

Cancers are enlightened souls who experience life by feeling everything deeply. You reach out to others, which can become too overwhelming. So you can get a little crabby, not because you enjoy being moody but because the feelings well up, and you're stuck trying to deal with them!

| LEO | FIRE | JULY 23–AUGUST 22 |

Ruling Planet: The Sun

Lucky Day: Sunday

Famous Leos: Robert De Niro, Napoleon, Madonna

Best Traits: You have so much enthusiasm and confidence that people are drawn to you. No matter what you do, somehow you always come out a winner.

Biggest Problems: Your larger-than-life personality can make you a tad bossy at times. If you are in a lazy mood, you try to get others to do things for you.

Trademark: "Who said the *Sun* was the center of the universe?"

Best Job: President.

Worst Job: Anything behind the scenes.

What You Love: Expensive meals, top-of-the-line pampering.

What You Hate: Disloyal friends and followers.

Best Way to Make a Million Bucks: Being a movie star.

Best Way to Spend a Million Bucks: Renting a plane and spending all of your money on one blowout party for 100 of your closest friends.

Your Secret Desire: Wanting all 100 of them to recognize you as royalty.

Best Gift to Give You: A golden crown.

Radiant, loyal, and impulsive, you are the kings and queens of the stars. Regal Leos do everything with pride and confidence. The problem is that sometimes you set up nearly impossible tasks for yourself—and then want immediate results. You get a bit self-centered.

Lavish spenders, Leos are the best at living large. Luxury is not a craving but a necessity for you. If you're going to do it, you might as well do it right! You love the three A's: attention, appreciation, and (most important) adoration. You are so cheery, loyal, and openhearted that your friends are willing to overlook the occasional bout of boasting or laziness. Let's face it: You love telling people what to do, but you do it so sincerely that it can actually be appealing.

Because you are a natural leader, motivating yourself to accomplish some of the detail-oriented tasks you wish to delegate can be hard. A little extra effort in that department will go a long way. This will have to be your own decision, though. Anyone trying to get you to do anything you don't want to do will make you roar.

Geminis like to be at the party, but Leos are best at *throwing* the party. Leos help themselves by helping others, and your always flamboyant, dramatic nature ensures that you'll be forever surrounded by admirers. You bring courage and warmth with you wherever you go. All you want is to be the center of attention!

VIRGO EARTH AUGUST 23–SEPTEMBER 22

Ruling Planet: Mercury

Lucky Day: Wednesday

Famous Virgos: Hugh Grant, Keanu Reeves, Claudia Schiffer

Best Traits: You're great at rearranging and perfecting things. Your practical, intelligent nature makes you a keeper to friends who need to get things done.

Biggest Problems: You can get so wrapped up in analyzing a situation that you forget your emotional side. Your X-ray vision can make you come across as critical.

Trademark: "Okay, so I am a little controlling. Big deal!"

Best Job: Computer engineer, TV producer.

Worst Job: Stuntperson, scuba diver.

What You Love: Fulfilling your constant need to be moving by organizing and reorganizing everything you come across.

What You Hate: Loud, disrespectful slobs.

Best Way to Make a Million Bucks: Micromanaging every detail for the largest company you can find.

Best Way to Spend a Million Bucks: Getting every sheet, towel, curtain, rug; every piece of furniture, every drop of paint, and every picture on the wall in your home to match perfectly.

Your Secret Desire: To be the Martha Stewart of the business world.

Best Gifts to Give You: Gift certificates. You're so high-maintenance that you'd much rather pick out things you want.

Virgos are detail-oriented perfectionists. Watch out! You can get so confused about what you should be fixing and what you shouldn't be fixing that you get into trouble sometimes. You have a tendency to organize your way right through other people's boundaries. You are great at finishing projects, planning vacations, and setting up offices. Instinctively, the first thing you do when you enter a new situation is to micromanage your way into being indispensable.

You love getting wrapped up in small details, such as alphabetizing your CD collection—other signs of the zodiac won't even notice all that earnest effort. But that's okay, since you have to do something with all that energy. But your attention to detail can be your downfall in the end: You imagine imperfections in yourself and others that are really not there.

For people born under this sign, trusting your emotions can be difficult. You are such a thinker, so analytical, that your feelings and emotions cloud your judgment and that of others. You are intolerant of people who make decisions based on their emotions. You go purely on the facts and think everyone else should, too.

Virgos always know a lot. Anyone can ask you anything—especially if the question is of a practical nature. You know every grocery, restaurant, drugstore, pet store, and flower shop within a five-mile radius, as well as their operating hours. This can get you into trouble. You love to give advice, but you don't take it well: A perfectionist doesn't need perfecting.

Virgos are caring people who often devote their life to service to others. You are also workaholics and worriers whose need for security outweighs the need to play. Give yourself a break—you may be missing out on some of the fun!

| LIBRA | AIR | SEPTEMBER 23–OCTOBER 22 |

Ruling Planet: Venus
Lucky Day: Friday
Famous Libras: Michael Douglas, Toni Braxton, Gwyneth Paltrow

Best Traits: You're a gracious listener, a charming and people-pleasing friend.

Biggest Problems: When you give, you expect to receive. This makes your interest in others seem self-serving.

Trademark: "We'll get along fine; just don't deny me any privileges I deserve."

Best Job: Diplomat, interior decorator.

Worst Job: Anything in which you have to get dirty.

What You Love: Beautiful refined art, music, and people.

What You Hate: When things in life are unfair.

Best Way to Make a Million Bucks: Sharing your beautiful visions of love and elegance with others.

Best Way to Spend a Million Bucks: Surrounding yourself and your mate with serene beauty.

Your Secret Desire: To be cradled in the lap of luxury, showered with adoration, and charm people for a living.

Best Gift to Give You: Dinner for two at the most exquisite restaurant you can find.

Libras are so social and easy to be around that you are guaranteed a large circle of friends and paramours. An air sign, you are intelligent and communicative by nature, and because the Scales are the zodiac's sign of partnerships, you thrive as one half of a team—in work, play, and love.

You aim to live your life in balance and harmony on every level, from your home environment to your work life to your relationships. You find others' actions intimidating if they threaten your Libran balance, and you rarely let anyone throw your emotions off kilter. Your strong sense of inner preservation and your desire to avoid conflict always keep you cool as a cucumber.

Ruled by Venus, you have an eye for all things beautiful and refined. Libras are always the best-dressed people at the party, but you tend to judge others by appearance alone. Another of your many talents: You are great at spending money. Beautiful things cost a lot, but there is nothing you hate more than having to do without something you feel you deserve.

Everyone associates the Scales with law and justice, but Libra's fine taste and artistic nature also lead you to careers in the fine arts, designing, decorating, and architecture. The bottom line: Basically you can do anything you want. If your skills and talents don't get you there, your charm definitely will.

SCORPIO WATER OCTOBER 23–NOVEMBER 22

Ruling Planet: Pluto

Lucky Day: Tuesday

Famous Scorpios: Pablo Picasso, Leonardo Di-Caprio, Puff Daddy

Best Trait: Wherever you go, whatever you do, your intense insight gives you a great awareness of what's going on beneath the surface.

Biggest Problem: Your fabulous creativity can get the best of you, because you imagine slights that are just not there or create situations in which you become brooding or jealous.

Trademarks: "You talking to *me*?" "Go ahead, make my day."

Best Jobs: Conspiracy theorist, criminal profiler.

Worst Jobs: Flight attendant, accountant.

What You Love: Getting into deep philosophical discussions about the mysteries of the universe, death, and reincarnation. Going to the extreme.

What You Hate: Being taken advantage of—you never forgive and forget.

Best Way to Make a Million Bucks: Using your powers as a visionary and starting your own cutting-edge business.

Best Way to Spend a Million Bucks: Climbing Mount Everest, jumping out of an airplane, circling the globe searching for the meaning of life.
Your Secret Desire: To right all the wrongs of humankind.
Best Gift to Give You: Ouija board.

The best two words that describe a Scorpio are *deep* and *extreme*. As a water sign, you are intuitive, compassionate, and emotional. But Scorpios get their insight and experience from the depths of the unconscious. Whether you realize it or not, you strive to awaken the hidden meanings and potentials in everything you do.

Scorpions are complex creatures. You are sensitive and strong-willed, independent and possessive, emotionally sharing and private, fearless and controlled—all at the same time. Other signs may wonder how it is possible to be so many contradictory things at once, but you inspire others to reach their depths and are often a positive force for those around you.

The most compelling and intense sign of the zodiac, you live your life channeling the infinite powers of the universe. Don't be surprised if others shy away from you, Scorpio. Your ability to penetrate whatever you are doing can be a bit intimidating—but then again, you wouldn't have it any other way!

You will be a powerhouse in your career, setting tremendous goals and accomplishing them with amazing persistence and concentration. Your ability to turn adversity into good fortune is one of your finest skills. You'll never waste your money on things you feel are unimportant—you will always have it to spend on your other worldly pursuits.

SAGITTARIUS   FIRE   NOVEMBER 22–DECEMBER 21

Ruling Planet: Jupiter

Lucky Day: Thursday

Famous Sagittarians: Tina Turner, Kenneth Branagh, Brad Pitt

Best Traits: You have a cheerful and optimistic nature and an infectious, carefree attitude.

Biggest Problems: You're so busy focusing on the big picture that you don't make time for deep personal communications and commitments.

Trademark: "I'm going to go find out if the grass is really greener over there."

Best Job: News anchor, astronaut.

Worst Job: Data processor.

What You Love: Telling stories; enthusiastically explaining your philosophy of life.

What You Hate: Being trapped in the same schedule day after day.

Best Way to Make a Million Bucks: Working in the media and communications: TV, radio, publishing, and the Internet.

Best Way to Spend a Million Bucks: Keep tons of it in your pockets at all times. You never know when you're going to want to give it away, take a trip, or buy yourself something really expensive.

Your Secret Desire: To have all the riches of life and not be tied down to any responsibilities.

Best Gifts to Give You: Cool travel books; skydiving lessons.

Sagittarians are explorers and philosophers, always seeking to learn new things and expand your awareness. You are the ultimate adventurer. To you life is a big journey and you're out to experience it all. In fact, you are such a fun-loving free spirit that the mere thought of straightening out and settling down has you feeling trapped. You can just imagine how other people feel when they try to get you to keep appointments and deadlines!

As a friend Archers are generous, openhearted, and fun to be around. You're always there to lend a hand, and you give with no strings attached. You'd give away your last dime to a friend in need and not expect anything in return.

You have a great ability to pick things up and let them go, so nothing holds you back. You believe in living in the moment. Nothing is worth doing unless you go all the way. You don't interfere in other people's lives—you definitely don't want them interfering in yours.

All this fiery freedom does have a bad side. You can't commit, so it's hard for you to stay in one place for very long, let alone to work at one job or to get married for a lifetime. You can be irresponsible and are chronically late for everything. And to top it off, as a philosopher, you get insulted when people misunderstand you. None of this is too serious, though. Your sense of humor and your honest and giving nature win out every time.

CAPRICORN   EARTH   DECEMBER 22–JANUARY 19

Ruling Planet: Saturn
Lucky Day: Saturday
Famous Capricorns: Joan of Arc, Tiger Woods, Kate Moss
Best Traits: You're so clever and patient, you'll wait for the perfect opportunity to strike even if it takes forever. You believe in yourself and your abilities.

Biggest Problems: If your feelings are hurt, you will secretly hold a grudge and let the resentment build until you explode!

Trademark: "Show me the money."

Best Job: Managing huge amounts of money.

Worst Job: Psychologist, social worker.

What You Love: Cultivating a shining reputation in your career.

What You Hate: Giving up too soon.

Best Way to Make a Million Bucks: Wheeling and dealing other people's money.

Best Way to Spend a Million Bucks: You'd never spend a million bucks.

Your Secret Desire: To win every time.

Best Gifts to Give You: Picture-in-picture TV, so you can watch CNN and MSNBC at the same time.

Capricorns do everything with purpose and authority. Every goal is pursued with the utmost determination. Every effort is packed with the desire for success, accomplishment, and status. With you, everything is serious business. Unlike Sagittarians and Geminis, you'd never take anything lightly—that includes a trip to the grocery store.

Goats have street smarts. You are great at sizing up a situation, figuring out all the angles, making the best preparations—and then working your way straight to the top. This concentration and determination helps Goats to achieve whatever they de-sire—career status, love, and of course, a full bank account.

Something most people don't know about you: Loyal, dependable Capricorns love to be appreci-ated. When you commit to someone or something, you're in it for the long haul. You're devoted to those in your inner circle, and your friends know they can count on you even in the toughest situation. The problem is that your emotions get hidden by your self-reliance, pride, and overwhelming determina-tion to succeed. Because you cherish security, your actions can make you appear cold or materialistic.

You are into accomplishments. You'd rather finish projects and receive accolades for your achievements than waste time in idle conversation. The rest of the zodiac can socialize. You've got way more important things to do!

AQUARIUS   AIR   JANUARY 20–FEBRUARY 18

Ruling Planet: Uranus
Lucky Day: Wednesday
Famous Aquarians: Jennifer Jason-Leigh, Baby Spice, Abraham Lincoln

Best Traits: You're an intellectual visionary, always on the cutting edge of the future. You have great powers of persuasion.

Biggest Problems: You're so opinionated that you get defensive too easily when narrow-minded people don't get you. You can be suspicious of emotions.

Trademark: "I refuse to march with the band—I like the music in my head much better."

Best Job: Inventor, Nobel Prize–winning scientist.

Worst Job: Office manager.

What You Love: Unconventional fame and glory.

What You Hate: Small-minded conservatives.

Best Way to Make a Million Bucks: Thinking up ways to save the universe.

Best Way to Spend a Million Bucks: Thinking up ways to save the universe.

Your Secret Desire: To be as big in life as others believe you are.

Best Gifts to Give You: The latest computer gadgets and software.

Aquarians see everything in life through unorthodox glasses. You're a progressive philosopher, an intelligent and idealistic visionary. You live in your mind, so you're a better thinker than a doer. You love to improve the world, but dislike putting in the required daily effort and energy. Your role is to create, and you let other people make your creations a reality.

One of your greatest strengths is your independence. You follow your heavenly inspiration and bravely try paths that would be considered too risky by most standards. A total nonconformist, you go out of your way to do things differently, to strike out on your own, to stand out from the crowd. You have no tolerance for *average*.

People flock to the Waterbearer because of your humanitarianism. Not only are you friendly and outgoing, but you truly want to see others happy. You love to talk big about your career goals, your desires for love. Your ideas impress people, but they also impress you a tad too much for your own good.

You may love the world, but you will definitely fight with any small-minded person who gets in your way. You form your opinions from the loftiest reaches of the universe, but once they're cast, you'll stubbornly never change them.

Altruistic, humanitarian, futuristic, and fun— from now on, Aquarians are the ones to watch. As we enter the Age of Aquarius, these qualities are sure to make the world a better place.

| PISCES | WATER | FEBRUARY 19–MARCH 20 |

Ruling Planet: Neptune

Lucky Day: Friday

Famous Pisces: Cindy Crawford, Michelangelo, Drew Barrymore

Best Traits: You are so intuitive and metaphysical that you make a trip to the mall a mystical experience.

Biggest Problems: The combination of your overgenerous nature and your attraction to questionable characters causes you to be taken advantage of easily.

Trademark: "What do you mean, I have to go to work? Can't I just stay home and pretend I'm doing something?"

Best Job: Psychic, painter.

Worst Job: Financial analyst.

What You Love: Spending large amounts of time being romantic and dreamy.

What You Hate: Balancing your checkbook.

Best Way to Make a Million Bucks: You're much better at spending it than at earning it.

Best Way to Spend a Million Bucks: Just by living your life: eating, sleeping, playing, daydreaming, meditating, giving large sums to the needy, and taking in stray animals.

Your Secret Desire: To be taken care of and never have to worry about small stuff like paying your rent and electric bill.

Best Gifts to Give You: Anything having to do with angels.

Pisces are the most agreeable, compassionate, and psychic people in the universe. The last sign of the zodiac, the Fish has a small part of all the others within its makeup, creating a connection to all that is.

Ruled by Neptune, the watery planet of the underworld, you truly understand the depths of the soul. Swimming along in a never-ending sea, you're adaptable, changeable, fickle, indecisive. It's hard for you to distinguish the boundaries between you and those around you. Easily influenced by your environment, you get confused by your emotions, not knowing which are really yours and which belong to someone else.

You're a great healer, and you choose your friendships wisely. In all of your relationships you seek the ultimate connection of body, mind, and spirit. You're romantic, sentimental, and kind, but insecure about everything. Deeply artistic and mysterious, you always seem to have a certain amount of drama swirling around you.

Pisces hate reality. You shy away from harsh working environments, choosing instead careers in the theater, fine arts, and psychology. You can easily get caught up in life's illusions: procrastinating, sleeping late, staying up all night watching your favorite movies. You're a denial expert.

Spiritual, ethereal Pisces is the zodiac's link to another dimension, but exactly where that is, nobody knows.

CHAPTER 3

Astro-Analyzing Your Sweethearts, Friends, and Parents

In this chapter you get to delve into others' thoughts, motivations, and actions. These twelve sections, one for each zodiac sign, focus on the characteristics of the people you know—parents, friends, and sweethearts.

ARIES   FIRE   MARCH 21–APRIL 19

The Aries Sweetheart: Sparks and Fireworks

If you have an Aries love interest, you've got your hands full. These hot-blooded pioneers are always looking for excitement. Their intense passion for life and love can be exhausting if they have no other outlet for their energy. They're outgoing, loving, and loyal. They can also be aggressive and determined. When they want something, they go after it with charm and gusto—if you don't know this already, you will. You simply cannot say no to an Aries pursuer.

Perfect date: Challenge your date to a game of pool, play a good game, then let your date win.

Best conversation topic: Your date's goals, desires, and fantasies for your relationship.

The Aries Friend: One Wild Ride

Aries friends love action, and since they enjoy being the center of attention, a constant flow of friends and supporters doesn't hurt either. They love to inspire others to move forward. Full of enthusiasm, they jump headfirst into new experiences. To them, this is just life, not impulsiveness. Aries are opinionated and independent. They set goals and go after them with a vengeance—with or without you! Aries friends are always fun to be around. You just need common interests and goals to keep their attention.

Best thing to do with an Aries buddy: Follow them around, doing whatever they want.

The Aries Parent: The Ultimate Authority

Dealing with Aries parents is not easy. They love to do what they want to do, and to project their desires onto their kids. On the other hand, they are full of zest and love life. They're on a big adventure, and want to share it with their children. They want their children to be independent, goal-minded individuals. It gets tricky when they say they want you to have an opinion of your own: It just can't go against theirs— there is simply no room. Establish some give-and-take within this relationship, and you can expect fireworks and fun.

Best way to get what you want from an Aries parent: If they don't want you to do something, short of praying, there's little you can do but suck it up and go their way.

TAURUS   EARTH   APRIL 20–MAY 20

The Taurus Sweetheart: The Practical Romantic

Physical, tender, and down-to-earth, Bulls make wonderful partners—that is, if you can handle their possessiveness. Beware: If you're looking for a fling, keep looking; *casual* is a word they just don't understand. They would rather not get involved unless they know it will last. Being in love brings out the best in Taurus. Their generosity and energy will always be focused in your direction; just don't try to control them, because their strong will and independent streak make that impossible. Attracting a Taurus takes extra effort. This is someone who needs a bit of coaxing to surrender to love.

Perfect date: A home-cooked meal, a horseback-riding lesson.

Best conversation topic: Money, business, possessions.

The Taurus Friend: A Loyal Companion

A friend in need can always count on the loyalty and generosity of a Bull. Need someone to help you build or move something? Call a Taurus—they're great at designing and constructing things. Need to borrow a few bucks? You guessed it: Call a Taurus. Just remember to pay them back—they like to please others, but they have a good memory! Taurus friends are great to hang out with, but only when they want to hang out. The truth about those friendly Bulls: They like their privacy as much as they like company. If you get them on a bad day, though, they can be a bit intolerant and obstinate.

Best things to do with a Taurus buddy: Go in-line skating or biking in the park, or organize a weekend car wash for extra cash.

The Taurus Parent: The Dependable Provider

Taurus moms and dads create stable, safe homes for their children. They're protective without being suffocating. On one hand, they lavish love and adoration on their children, but on the other hand, they won't let you get away with anything. They're big on independence and self-reliance, teaching you to take responsibility for yourself. Do your chores and get a part-time job. They'll show you how to be practical with the money you make.

They enjoy doing outdoorsy things with you like camping, hiking, and picnicking. If you want something your way, be prepared to state your case with good reasons and possibly an argument. Once Taurus parents have made up their minds, it is hard to get them to change—especially when they are in the driver's seat.

Best way to get what you want from a Taurus parent: Genuine appreciation and validation. Thank them for doing things for you, for having your best interest at heart. Let them know you appreciate their point of view.

GEMINI   AIR   MAY 21–JUNE 20

The Gemini Sweetheart: He Loves Me, He Loves Me Not

Geminis are charming, and they genuinely love people. They're great talkers and like to keep things light. That makes them fun dates, but once the honeymoon is over, so might be the relationship. Their minds are so quick that they have little patience, and when there is even a hint of boredom, they're gone. Geminis have to work at slowing down and looking deeper. Once they do, they're great at forgiving and forgetting, planning fun experiences, and experimenting with life's pleasures.

Perfect date: Going to the hottest dance club, people-watching.

Best conversation topic: Fun stories, gossip—a little of everything.

The Gemini Friend: Socially Skilled

Geminis are a lot of fun to be around. They know something about everything and tell stories with flair. With their energetic and witty personality they are great at whipping up intimate groups of friends as only a true air sign can. If you've had a bad day, talk to a Gemini: They'll tell you something funny, lifting you up in no time. Gemini friends are talkative. They can chat it up about movies, current events, the latest sites on the Internet. They always know who's cheating and which couple is breaking up. If you tell them something, don't be surprised if it ends up in one of their funny stories.

Best thing to do with a Gemini buddy: Go for coffee or brunch and let them talk to you about everything they know.

The Gemini Parent: An Entertaining Authority

Gemini parents can actually be fun, playing and laughing a lot. They also have the attention span of a kid in a candy store. They respect their children's unique personalities and enjoy dressing them up and taking them wherever they go. Gemini parents can be so light and airy with their children that it's hard for them to say no. Gemini moms and dads like to play lots of mind games, board games, and trivia games, and they have a fast and direct approach to teaching their children new skills. They also like to accept things at face value and might not get deep enough into their kids' heads to understand what's really going on inside.

Best way to get what you want from a Gemini parent: Just ask. If there's a way to give it to you, they'll definitely figure it out.

| CANCER | WATER | JUNE 21–JULY 22 |

The Cancer Sweetheart: A Sentimental Love

Cancers are sweet and loving, but they send you such subtle signs that you have to be on the lookout for the unspoken clues. Although cautious at first, they love to be in love and are romantic and affectionate. After you have won their heart, you will constantly get little gifts, tokens of their affection. Just don't mess with their feelings—once hurt, they're gone for good. They may take you back, but no amount of apologizing will make them forget.

If you're too independent to commit to just one person, skip the Crab. They're a bit clingy, can get jealous, and need a lot of reassurance at times. Want to attract a Cancer? Show them how affectionate, loving, and sentimental you can be. They love to dream up romantic scenarios. Play along and create one together!

Perfect date: Surprise them with tickets to the ballet, or find out what their favorite restaurant is and take them there.

Best conversation topic: Tell them about a personal problem that is bothering you. Compliment them on what great listeners they are!

The Cancer Friend: Half Friend, Half Therapist

If you want to surround yourself with sympathetic and caring people, you have found the perfect playmates in the Crab. When they feel safe, they are devoted friends, and they stay that way for a long, long time. Once you have penetrated their shell, Cancers are loving forever. No matter how far apart you may be, Cancer friends always keep you near and dear to their heart. Cancer friends need a lot of love and support in return, and a good friendship can help them overcome their fears and spread their wings.

Don't lie to a Cancer. They're masters at understanding people and will pick up on the tiniest of clues. They're also great at anticipating public opinion. Keep them around if you're running for captain or president. With their insight on your side, you'll come out a winner.

Best thing to do with a Cancer buddy: Spend a lazy afternoon remembering old times.

The Cancer Parent: An Overprotective and Understanding Nurturer

Many astrologers say that Cancers make the best parents—that is, as long as they keep their overbearing tendencies in check. Cancers are natural nurturers, creating the most loving environment a child could ask for. Their sensitivity and compassion allows them to really understand what is going on in your head. The only problem is their inconsistent moods. If they've had a bad day, you'll know it. They can also be big worriers. They won't let you in on this, but they often wonder if they are doing the right thing by you. They always have lots of stuff going on beneath the surface and one foot in the past. The key to figuring out their motivation is to uncover all that underlying stuff they're not telling you.

Best way to get what you want from a Cancer parent: Pour your heart out and give them all the emotional reasons you want to do what you want to do. Give them a hug.

LEO   FIRE   JULY 23–AUGUST 22

The Leo Sweetheart: Over the Top!

Affairs of the heart are larger than life in the eyes of Leos. Intense and passionate, they love being showered with affection and having their every whim catered to—they are royalty, don't forget. They're searching for the mythic princess or white knight, creating a love of huge proportions—until reality strikes and they realize that you are just a human after all. Yes, they're domineering and like to have things their way, but don't be too wishy-washy—they find an equal partner much more fulfilling.

Perfect date: Roll out the red carpet and take them out for a fun-filled day of romance and excitement.

Best conversation topic: Them, of course!

The Leo Friend: The Ringleader

Outgoing, approachable Leos make wonderful friends. Their big egos make them demanding, but their desire to please others makes them cooperative and understanding. They truly care about the welfare of friends and family, and are ready to lend a hand, even if that means directing the effort from high above the crowds. Everyone loves a Leo, and Leos love attention—a perfect combination. Their personalities are as big as the Sun, and their warmth is as comforting as a toasty fire. Just watch their roar on a bad day. They can get aggressive and disagreeable.

Best thing to do with a Leo buddy: Go to a social event and let them hold court.

The Leo Parent: Creatively Extravagant

Leos create a safe, loving place in which to grow, but they won't hesitate to remind you who is really in control. They want you to be able to go after what you want with courage and ambition, but don't talk back to them. They value honesty and respect, and will always remember the time when they didn't get it. Proud Leo parents love a good party, so your birthday bashes are probably the biggest in the neighborhood—not to mention the loudest. Just don't expect the spotlight to shine only on you. Leos always manage to grab some for themselves—they can't help it.

Best way to get what you want from a Leo parent: Let them know how much you adore and appreciate them. Straightforwardly ask for what you want, and then thank them profusely when you get it.

Virgo Earth   August 23–September 22

The Virgo Sweetheart: The Reserved Romantic

A Virgo love is characterized by a disciplined passion, conservative and controlled, yet delicate and sensitive. Virgos carry a torch for true love. Above all, they search for a lasting love, someone they can care for and protect. They respect and appreciate their mates, saving their tenderness for private moments. They like to do things for their sweethearts. Give them a key to your apartment and you'll come home one day to find a fabulous dinner waiting. Most of the time, Virgos' emotions are cool and contained, but watch out: Occasionally they can bubble over and blow like an active volcano.

Perfect date: A trip to a museum. Just make sure you can discuss the art in detail.

Best conversation topic: Career, money, investments, and current events.

The Virgo Friend: The Perfect Planner

Virgos fit in best with intimate groups of similar friends. Not much for idle chatter, they like to zero in on sensible topics and discuss them in depth. They're loyal and love to help you with anything and everything—even if you don't ask. Reorganizing your closet, moving your furniture, planning a party—these are things Virgos love to discuss and assist with. They're so detailed and practical that when they offer advice, sometimes they can come off as a bit critical. Beware: Virgos take things personally. They are so precise that they put everything you say under a microscope.

Best thing to do with a Virgo buddy: Shop for that perfect hard-to-find sweater.

The Virgo Parent: The Detailed Doer

Families with Virgo parents have the most organized homes and take the best-planned vacations. Not very spontaneous, they're great at setting a schedule and sticking to it. You can count on them to create a stable and solid foundation on which to grow. With a Virgo mom or dad, you will always know what is expected of you—and it's usually a lot! They're perfectionists, but they always do a lot for their children, filling up their days with activities and chaperoning them everywhere. Don't be surprised if some of those activities are work and chores, though. Virgos hold personal responsibility in high esteem.

Best way to get what you want from a Virgo parent: Give them a well-thought-out plan, complete with pros and cons.

LIBRA AIR SEPTEMBER 23–OCTOBER 22

The Libra Sweetheart: Full of Charm

Libras are captivating and charming. They love being desired and desirable. With Venus as a ruler, would you expect anything else? Their favorite thing about love is old-fashioned romance. They will sweep you off your feet until you give in to their enchanting elegance. Libras' search for balance can sometimes stop them from exploring. They'd prefer to stay calm and composed rather than get into a messy emotional scene. Although they seek partnership, lifetime commitment doesn't come easily to Libras. That changes, though: After a few years playing the field, they're more than happy to form a lasting partnership.

Perfect date: A Broadway musical and a sophisticated supper.

Best conversation topic: Each other. Flirt your heart out; they'll love it!

The Libra Friend: The Social Butterfly

Libras love being friends. Social contacts are very important to them. Being sociable is in their astrological blood. They're diplomatic, open-minded, aloof, and adaptable. They're more likely to go along with the crowd rather than to make a scene or go it alone. Their need for balance leaves no room for risk. Well educated, intelligent, creative, and artistic, they enjoy talking about high-minded subjects with other intelligent and artistic people. They host the perfect party—from their decorations, to the perfect food and drink, to their outfit. Libras are good for everyone's self-esteem: They're great at giving compliments and making you feel like a million bucks!

Best thing to do with a Libra buddy: Go to a fancy club where they can indulge their fine taste and talk for hours about their philosophy.

The Libra Parent: Fairness to the Max

Libra moms and dads are likable and easygoing people—that is, until you question their authority. Top on their priority list: They believe they deserve the utmost respect from their children. When they don't get it, they're more likely to shut down than blow up, but either way, you're out of luck. Libra parents are easily swayed. They may say no at first, but ask them a few more times and they're likely to give in. Beware, though: They do tally things up. If they give in this time, they'll expect you to give in the next. When making decisions, Libra parents weigh all the facts and make their choices based on their intellect and reasoning—or they leave the decision to the other parent.

Best way to get what you want from a Libra parent: Give them the pros and cons, make your case well, and whatever you do, don't get overemotional.

SCORPIO   WATER
OCTOBER 23–NOVEMBER 21

The Scorpio Sweetheart: Intensely Passionate

Romance with a Scorpio is full of intensity, excitement, and mystery. You never know when explosions will erupt and spontaneity will overtake reason. You may have headed out for burgers on the corner, but you could end up eating in the next state. Scorpio sweethearts are very demanding: They expect 100 percent of your time and attention. It's worth it, though. In return you get passion, emotion, and romance. Anyone involved with Scorpios knows not to get on their bad side. They become so vulnerable in love that when they are hurt, they can't help but lash out and sting you. They're also prone to fits of jealousy, deserved or not.

Perfect date: Snag the back table in a dark after-hours club and talk all night.

Best conversation topic: The depths and secrets of human nature.

The Scorpio Friend: Ultimate and Extreme

Scorpios are intense people. One look tells you there's a Scorpio in your midst. They have deep, piercing eyes, an expressive smile, and a passionate glow about them. They're as deep in life as they are in looks. If you have a Scorpio friend, then you already know that they never play it safe. Scorpios have that all-or-nothing vibe with their friends, too, expecting commitment and honesty—and nothing less. They notice everything, even what's going on inside, and they'll be sure to let you know it. If you're doing a project with Scorpios, you'd better leave them in charge. They have intense willpower, and will precisely plan and execute the entire project, down to the tiniest detail.

Best thing to do with a Scorpio buddy: Go to a carnival, ride the scariest rides, and visit the haunted house.

The Scorpio Parent: The Idealistic Protector

Scorpio parents have an intense need to know the depths of their kids' souls. All that focus on you makes for an embrace that is devoted, affectionate, smothering, and controlling, all at the same time. There's never a dull moment in a Scorpio house. Their children will have an understanding of philosophy and compassion. When they play, they want to take their children on the biggest slide in the park. If you have a Scorpio parent, you'd better not do anything devious. They're the best at uncovering mysteries and hidden secrets. They're also not the most emotionally stable parents—outbursts and eruptions are normal.

Best way to get what you want from a Scorpio parent: Appeal to their sense of adventure and their heartfelt emotions.

SAGITTARIUS FIRE
NOVEMBER 22–DECEMBER 21

The Sagittarius Sweetheart: No Strings Attached

Sagittarians love to flirt, explore, and play with everyone. Sagittarians never take anything too seriously. They make commitments to the moment. When they say "I love you" they mean it, but that doesn't mean they'll stick around forever. Getting a Sagittarius to commit takes a unique combination of ingredients: You need the same interests in philosophy, sports, and activities; a desire for freedom and travel; and a cool sense of humor. If you commit to a Sag, you'll find yourself always moving and exploring the world. Archers are generous, forgiving, and never jealous. They like to maintain friendships with their old flames and leave the door open to the possibility of future flirting.

Perfect date: Let them decide. Overplanning can bring out the committment-phobe in them.

Best conversation topic: Where to go and what to do during your next vacation.

The Sagittarius Friend: The Ultimate Enthusiast

Sagittarius folks have a wide variety of friends in a wide variety of places. They have friends they travel with, and friends they talk with over coffee, and friends they meet on the basketball court playing a pickup game. They hop, skip, and jump from one activity to the next, perking up everyone they come in contact with. They dislike deep emotional entanglements and will joke their way out of them rather than tackle them head-on. They're always coming up with big plans for themselves. They achieve their goals with a bit of discipline and a bit of luck (which is always on their side!) and promptly move on to the next goal, sailing through life like it's one big adventure.

Best thing to do with a Sagittarius buddy: A fun day of outdoor adventure and activity.

The Sagittarius Parent: Freedom for Everyone

Growing up with a Sagittarius parent is a big adventure. Children of Sagittarians are always surrounded by friends and family, travel often, and learn to think for themselves at an early age. Sag parents are likely to have offbeat jobs that take them to interesting places. They are torn between taking their children along to expose them to life, and leaving them home during their odd hours on the job. Archers love their children but need their freedom, too. They'll be sure to have a list of baby-sitters and grandparents around in case they get the urge for a taste of freedom. Sagittarian moms and dads are spontaneous, easygoing, and caring, and they never stick to a schedule. You might never know what the next moment brings, but you can be sure it'll be full of fun.

Best way to get what you want from a Sagittarius parent: They are lenient when it comes to freedom, so you don't even have to ask—just do it and be responsible.

CAPRICORN EARTH
DECEMBER 22–JANUARY 19

The Capricorn Sweetheart: Concealed Affection

The Capricorn in love is romantic in a practical way. They take responsibility for their mate's happiness, planning out their lives together, from where they will live to what they will do. If security is what you crave, Capricorns are the best providers. The problem is that they have everything planned out, and there's no room for spontaneity. If you don't fit their ideal, they may decide they're better off without you. Capricorns look for lasting love. They take their time, size up a potential mate, and figure out if the relationship will work before they act. On the outside Goats are confident and emotionally reserved. They need their significant others to appreciate them—even if they don't show it. When they feel comfortable and safe, they are loving and giving partners.

Perfect date: Go to a good lecture. Then go out for an evening of good food and conversation.

Best conversation topic: Money, career opportunities.

The Capricorn Friend: Patient Leadership

Capricorns are great at getting things done and doing a perfect job in the process. Because they're so success-driven, at times they can seem shy and detached, but their feelings are just hidden behind that cool exterior. They take everything seriously and don't like to waste their time on trivia. Don't ask them to spend a day shopping or sitting around watching football; these aren't activities they enjoy.

They'd rather be out accomplishing things. Capricorns are devoted and loyal friends who like to surround themselves with successful, bright, and educated people. They're not great at expressing their feelings, but are better at doing things for people they care about.

Best thing to do with a Capricorn buddy: Talk about your goals and about how you plan to make tons of money in the future.

The Capricorn Parent: A Secure Upbringing

You can count on Capricorn moms and dads to create a safe and secure home life, but it isn't going to be an easy ride—they're tough! They prize success for both themselves and their children. Capricorn parents don't readily show their emotions, but they give in other ways. Their children will have a good work ethic, will be independent, and will appreciate art and theater. Unfortunately, Capricorn parents are workaholics. If they work outside the home, you might not see them as much as you'd like. Above all, Capricorn parents need gratitude and recognition from their children. Deep down inside they are kind of insecure, and they need to know they're doing a good job at raising you.

Best way to get what you want from a Capricorn parent: Prove to them that you have made a wise decision based on good reasons, not emotions.

AQUARIUS   AIR
JANUARY 20–FEBRUARY 18

The Aquarius Sweetheart: Amorously Inventive

Aquarian loves are generous, patient, independent, and unconventional. They're imaginative, seeking to create the ideal mythical romantic adventure for both of you. They have so much going on in their heads that they tend to get a bit scattered, with everything they're involved in—including their love lives. On the other hand, that makes it easier to hide their emotions, and that's exactly the way they like to be: detached and distant. Don't make many demands on your Aquarians, and don't try to tie them down—that's the fastest way to lose your Waterbearers to the wind. Journey with an Aquarius through life's adventure and you'll find a mate who is intellectually stimulating, sociable, and unselfish.

Perfect date: Go to a foreign film or a poetry reading.

Best conversation topic: How to make the world a better place.

The Aquarius Friend: The World's Humanitarian

Aquarian pals are naturally sociable and like to hang out with a large and diverse group of friends. Intelligent Aquarians love to analyze, and they value their freedom. Their favorite place at the party is by the door—that way they can people-watch all night, chitchat with friends as they walk in, and leave when they've had enough. Waterbearers are restrained and independent. They'd rather work alone than ask for advice and get into a deep emotional encounter. They're progressive in their body, mind, and soul. From what they wear to what they say, Aquarians love dancing to their own drummer. Having an Aquarian friend will probably make you a better person, too. With an uncommon concern for the welfare of the world, they're the humanitarians of the Zodiac: caring, giving, and optimistic.

Best thing to do with an Aquarius buddy: Sit at Starbucks for hours talking about the latest technology and how it is going to change the world.

The Aquarius Parent: Offbeat and Airy

Aquarian parents are bright and playful. They believe in themselves and in their abilities as parents. Once they make a decision or take action, they never question or reevaluate. Emotionally, Aquarians aren't the most demonstrative sign in the universe. They have a cerebral warmth and prefer to keep things in cool balance. Their children have an empathy for the problems of the world. Aquarians are such fast thinkers that they have a tendency to jump to conclusions. If you discuss a deep problem or unresolved issue with them, they take a broad-minded and analytic approach to the solution.

Best way to get what you want from an Aquarius parent: They're so easygoing and respectful that if what you want is reasonable, they'll gladly give it to you.

PISCES   WATER
FEBRUARY 19–MARCH 20

The Pisces Sweetheart: Creative and Dreamy

All Pisces needs or wants is love and romance. They are sensual, mysterious, imaginative partners. The Fish excel at providing their sweethearts with exactly what they need. They love to create dreamy evenings in which you can whisper sweet nothings to each other. They love attention and affection: A Pisces in love can never give or get enough. The problem is that Pisces hate reality. You may wake up one day to see that what you have created won't work in the real world. Sometimes they can cross the line and go from love and affection to emotional neediness and dependence. If you like to step in and save the day, Pisces is the perfect love for you. Luckily their compassionate, spiritual, and supportive nature outweighs any shortcomings.

Perfect date: Ride a horse-drawn carriage and sip champagne.

Best conversation topic: Anything artistic and spiritual; your problems and feelings.

The Pisces Friend: Otherworldly Compassion

Pisces make soulful friends. A Pisces will listen for hours if you share your problems, and then will offer spiritual and optimistic wisdom. On the other hand, Pisces people can easily become overwhelmed with their own problems and need to lean on friends to get them through. Pisces are great at helping to make their friends' goals reality, often underestimating the power of their own creativity in the process. They're psychic, so don't be surprised if your Pisces friend reads your mind or finishes your sentences. Those born under the sign of the Fish can be insecure when it comes to making decisions, especially difficult ones. Reality is something they try to avoid whenever possible.

Best thing to do with a Pisces buddy: Read magazines with gorgeous Hollywood stars, and imagine which ones you'd marry.

The Pisces Parent: Intuitively Understanding

Pisces parents will give up anything to make sure their children have what they want and need. When Pisces become parents, their insecurities are magnified. They constantly call on their friends and family to make sure that what they're doing is best for the children. The slippery Fish have a hard time with discipline. The word *no* isn't in their vocabulary. It's not that they want to spoil you—they're just afraid of hurting your feelings. Don't expect a reality check from these folks. *Someone* must be cleaning the house and paying the bills around there—you just might not know who it is.

Best way to get what you want from a Pisces parent: Explain why what you want is good for your soul.

CHAPTER 4

To Be or Not to Be: Compatibility Between Signs

How compatible is your sign with the other signs of the zodiac? Look and see. Find the heading for your Sun sign, then read what it says about you and your romantic interests, parents, and friends, or anyone else you know.

Each relationship is rated one to four stars, depending upon the astrological positives and negatives between the two signs. The absolutely best combinations in the zodiac have a four-star rating. They have the most complementary character traits and desires. Keep in mind, though, that every great relationship also has a downside.

Three-star ratings signify very good compatibility. These relationships have many things in common as well as a few more disharmonious aspects than the four-star matches, but that makes life fun!

Even two-star pairings aren't bad: They have a 50/50 chance of success or failure. Very often the outcome of a relationship with two stars is determined by the additional astrological aspects that you will learn about in chapter 5, "Beyond the Basics": your Moon sign, and Mars and Venus placements.

A relationship rated one star is a toughie. The two people think, feel, and communicate differently. These are the long shots of the zodiac.

Friendships and parent/child relationships have different ratings because they are based on different ideals from those of romantic liaisons. Friends have mutual interests and common goals. The ratings for friends are based on how much they have in common. Parent/child relations are about love and caring, but also about family history, joint responsibilities, and unresolved issues. Getting along because we *want* to or because we *have* to are two different things. Some parent/child relationships are easier than others because of the characteristics of their astrological signs, and those are the ones with the higher star ratings.

ARIES   FIRE   MARCH 21–APRIL 19

Aries and Aries:
★ ★ Romance ★ ★ ★ Friends ★ ★ ★ Parent/Child

This starts off as a fine and fiery romance. Passionate and energetic, two Aries have a lot in common. You will have a blast together, but things may erupt because both of you like to be the leader. Is one of you going to give in? Doubt it!

Two Aries friends get along really well as long as each has a group to lead around. Parent/child Aries have a great time, although there are lots of emotional and physical outbursts. As the kid half of the relationship, don't expect to win very often.

Aries and Taurus:
★ Romance ★ ★ Friends ★ Parent/Child

If you are dating a Taurus, watch out! You get along on the physical level, but that's it. Think about it: Put a Ram and a Bull together and the only thing you're going to get is a big mess. You love freedom and spontaneity, but Taurus is slow-moving and possessive. Taurus' pace would drive you crazy.

Aries and Taurus friends get along much better. They do have a good time together, but it's best to stick to a small group. That way, others will be around to diffuse any difficulties. Aries/Taurus parent/child combinations are about as good as stale bread. You can have a lot of fun together but will butt heads a lot. You will end up the leader, but you won't be able to move Taurus anyway.

Aries and Gemini:
★ ★ ★ Romance ★ ★ ★ ★ Friends ★ ★ ★ Parent/Child

Aries and Gemini are both talkative, fun-loving, and energetic. Aries love their freedom, and so do Geminis. The difference is that you act before you think, and Geminis are so quick that they think before they act. To make this work, keep up on the latest fads, movies, and gossip. Both of you need constant stimulation.

This is one of the best pal combinations in the zodiac, providing you have similar interests, education, and intelligence. As parent/child, you are a fun and exciting pair. However, Gemini parents will get the last word—they actually talk more than you do!

Aries and Cancer:
★ Romance ★ ★ Friends ★ Parent/Child

Aries are full of spunk. Cancers are moody and sensitive. You would go nuts trying to pick up their spirit, and Cancers would be too easily hurt by your energetic outbursts. With this relationship, the small things lead to a lot of irritation on both sides.

Aries and Cancer friends get along okay, but if you get too close, you'll find you have two different styles, and neither of you will change. Parent/child Aries and Cancers survive because you have a lot of love for each other. Aries are always pushing for more, and that is where Cancerian defenses come in handy.

Aries and Leo:
★★★★Romance★★★★Friends★★★Parent/Child

These two fire signs are a great match: Both are passionate, generous, and enthusiastic. You and a Leo understand each other to the core. The only problem—and it's a biggie—is that you both have healthy egos. Neither one of you is going to roll over, but you need to find a way for both of you to split up the top job so that each is in charge of a different part of the relationship. This could end up as a wonderful combination.

The same goes for friendships and parent/child relationships. Fire signs in a bad mood can be stubborn and condescending, a problem for people living under the same roof. Give up your need to win or be first, and things will smooth over.

To Be or Not to Be

Aries and Virgo:
★ Romance ★ ★ Friends ★ Parent/Child

If you meet a Virgo, run for your life! You and a Virgo are one of the worst matches in the zodiac. You like to burst onto the scene with energy and passion. Virgos are reserved and like to check everything out before moving ahead. You look at the big picture, and Virgos are stuck on the details. You are extravagant, and Virgos are cautious. The only thing you have in common are the arguments.

Friends are a little luckier, because Aries enjoy coming up with far-fetched ideas, and Virgos enjoy making them reality. Parent/child Aries/Virgos talk apples and oranges. You need to be more patient, and Virgo needs to stop nitpicking.

Aries and Libra:
★ ★ Romance ★ ★ ★ Friends ★ ★ ★ Parent/Child

This is a romantic toss-up between two and three stars. The Moon, Venus, and Mars signs really make a difference here. On one hand, refined Libras could get annoyed at Aries gruffness. On the other hand, Aries' boundless energy can inspire Libras to get moving.

Aries/Libra friends are usually great together, except that if Libras are in the mood for calm surroundings, you need to back off. Aries and Libra family members also understand each other and communicate well.

Aries and Scorpio:
★Romance★ ★Friends★Parent/Child

These two get along like a stick of dynamite and a match. When these two powerful forces meet, they explode. You are both deeply passionate, forceful, opinionated, and domineering—it's just a matter of who will win this battle.

Friends in these signs work if you have mutual interests and a big enough pond to swim in. Parent/child Aries/Scorpios will have a lot of flare-ups. Someone will have to give in—be prepared.

Aries and Sagittarius:
★★★★Romance★★★★Friends★★★★Parent/Child

The Ram and the Archer are a match made in heaven. Both are forceful, lively, social, and have a great sense of humor. Both love freedom, adventure, and activity. All your fun and excitement is bound to keep a Sagittarian's flirty nature in balance. The one downfall: Your authoritative nature could make Sag squirm.

Aries/Sagittarius friends have so much fun together—too much fun, sometimes; it could get mere mortals running for the hills. Fire sign parents and children understand each other so well, you couldn't ask for a better combination.

Aries and Capricorn:
★ Romance ★ ★ Friends ★ Parent/Child

The Ram and the Goat are too stubborn to make it together in the real world. You are wild, extravagant, fun-loving. Capricorns are conservative with their time, their fun, and their money. They work, and you play. The only thing you have in common is that each of you thinks your lifestyle is the better of the two. When you meet Capricorns, introduce them to someone else!

Friendships between Aries and Capricorn rate two stars mainly because you don't have to live together—it's much easier to get along that way. Unfortunately, parents and children of this pairing have to navigate over some rough spots. It's a good thing you're both full of determination!

Aries and Aquarius:
★ ★ ★ Romance ★ ★ ★ ★ Friends ★ ★ ★ Parent/Child

Romances between Aries and Aquarius are generally very good. You both have adventurous spirits: Aries on the physical level, and Aquarius in the mind. You can create wild scenarios together and have a great time fulfilling them—you using your exuberance, and Aquarius using wit and wisdom. The obstacle here: Aquarians get lost in their quest for the meaning of life, and you can get quite whiny if you feel you aren't getting enough attention.

Aries and Aquarius friends are very supportive of each other, helping each achieve their goals and having fun too. Parents and children of this pairing usually get along well, too, except when you're looking to be the king or queen and Aquarians aren't in the mood to curtsy.

Aries and Pisces:
★ Romance ★ ★ Friends ★ Parent/Child

Aries and Pisces are good at flirting with each other—and the relationship should end right there. Pisces enjoy being uncovered like a well-wrapped gift, and you like to get right to the good stuff. You find Pisces indecisiveness boring, and Pisces find you emotionally grating.

Friendships between Aries and Pisces can be exciting and creative when Pisces are happy. If not, no matter how pushy you are, they're not going to snap out of it. Honestly, parent/child relations of this pairing are never easy. You may find your Pisces parent's neediness more than you can handle.

TAURUS   EARTH   APRIL 20–MAY 20

Taurus and Aries:
★ Romance ★ ★ Friends ★ Parent/Child

To an Aries, every day is a change for adventure—and you hate changes in your routine. Aries see what they want and immediately run off after it. You like to evaluate a situation before leaping. An Aries love would go crazy trying to get you moving, and you'd get really annoyed with the Aries' need to dominate. Face it: This isn't going to work for more than a minute.

Taurus/Aries friendships are fine as long as the Aries remembers that patience is a virtue. Parent/child relationships between Taurus and Aries don't work much better than the romances. You are a bit better at compromising than they are, as long as you don't think what they want is being forced on you.

Taurus and Taurus:
★ ★ ★ Romance ★ ★ ★ ★ Friends ★ ★ ★ ★ Parent/Child

Two Taureans together are quite stable. There are two big snags: The first is the possessive and jealous nature of the Bull—you will both need to chill out. Also, two slow-moving Taureans can get boring together—just how many days can you sit around and do nothing? Date a Taurus and you'll find out.

Friend and family relations between two Bulls are even better than romance. Your similar desires create common ground, and you can get your energy and excitement from the other members of the zodiac that you hang out with.

Taurus and Gemini:
★Romance★ ★Friends★ ★Parent/Child

As a rule, earth signs and air signs don't do much for each other. Your need for stability and Gemini's need for constant intellectual stimulation will probably end up driving you both nuts. You like to do everything slowly, and Geminis are quick on the draw. In the long run, Geminis are too fickle for your taste, and you are too single-minded for theirs!

Friendships between Taurus and Geminis can work out as long as you don't see each other for long stretches of time, but that's pretty much guaranteed—Geminis don't do anything for long amounts of time. Parent/child relationships are okay. You just can't count on Geminis to give you the stability you need.

Taurus and Cancer:
★★★★Romance★★★★Friends★★★Parent/Child

Matches between Taurus and Cancer are as close to perfect as you can get. You both love nothing more than to hang out with your mate all day. You need to be appreciated, and Cancers smother their partners with love and affection. Both Taureans and Cancers are possessive and jealous. You like to hold on to things, and Cancers don't like to let go of things. Just remember that Cancers are moody, so try to be as understanding as you can.

Taurus/Cancer friends match up perfectly as well, although you're more straightforward, and Cancers have everything going on under the surface. Parent/child pairings are a perfect fit, except that you both like staying home too much. If you're lucky, someone energetic will influence you to get out and experience life a little.

Taurus and Leo:
★Romance★★Friends★Parent/Child

The only thing that a Bull and a Lion do when they get together is compete. You're methodical and grounded, and Leos are fabulously flamboyant. You like attention, and they like even more attention. You're stubborn, and they're egotistical. There's nothing worse than the two of you trying to work this out. The more effort you both put in, the more hardheaded you'll become.

Taurus and Leo friends have more of a chance, especially if they're members of the same team—each with its own special responsibility, of course! The parent/child version of this is troublesome, too, with lots of butting heads and tugs-of-war. Good luck!

Taurus and Virgo:
★★★★Romance ★ ★ ★ Friends ★ ★ ★ Parent/Child

Taurus and Virgo loves both have a very good idea of what they want and how they want it done. It's a good thing that you both have the same desires in life: success and stability. Excitement and spontaneity are lacking here—but you could care less about that, anyway.

Earth sign friends get along like bread and butter. They have the same thoughts and feelings. Taurus and Virgo parent/child combinations are also based on mutual ideas, love, and respect. Just watch that you don't take the standard Virgo criticisms personally.

To Be or Not to Be

Taurus and Libra:
★★Romance★★★Friends★★Parent/Child

Taurus and Libra are both ruled by the love and beauty of Venus. Unfortunately, the two of you are destined for a short-lived romance. Libras are carefree in love, and ultimately that would drive you out of your bullish mind. You'd never feel like they were taking you or the relationship very seriously. Both of you are so relentless that disagreements would never come to a healthy conclusion.

Friendships will work as long as the Libra works on patience and you work on becoming more broad-minded. Parent/child Taurus/Libras will have the same appreciation of fine clothing, food, and decor. You are more conservative with love and money, but Libras can easily charm you out of it.

Taurus and Scorpio:
★★Romance★★★Friends★★Parent/Child

A Taurus and a Scorpio are two powerful signs. You are both willful, ambitious, possessive, and jealous. That could make for a wild ride. Together you'll get along either really well or really badly, depending upon how much effort you're both putting into communicating and working things out. If you both learn to be a bit more flexible and forgiving, there's hope.

Friends of this pairing connect well—particularly when you're trying to achieve the same goals. Parent/child Taurus/Scorpios might fight some hot-blooded battles. The combination is intense, and sometimes you may feel that there's not enough room for both of you.

Taurus and Sagittarius:
★ Romance ★ Friends ★ Parent/Child

Taureans and Sagittarians are totally different. You never do anything without first thinking of the consequences, while the Archer has a happy-go-lucky attitude toward life. What pleases you would bore them, and what excites them would frazzle you. When you meet Sagittarians tell them you're already taken.

Taurus/Sagittarius friends aren't going to do well either. They like each other well enough, but their interests are so different that they don't have enough in common. Parents and children of these signs get along better than friends or romantic partners because they have to, not because it comes easy.

To Be or Not to Be

Taurus and Capricorn:
★★★★Romance★★★★Friends★★★Parent/Child

Taurus people can't find a better match than a Capricorn. You both love to sit for hours contemplating the details of your successes. You both have unbeatable determination and loyalty. There's not much fun, excitement, or spontaneity going on, but you don't want loud, raucous fun, anyway—so what's the difference?

Earthly friends communicate well, seeing eye to eye on a lot of stuff. Taurus and Capricorn family members have comfortable and easygoing relationships. The only problem is: Who will get them to stop taking everything so seriously and lighten up?

Taurus and Aquarius:
★Romance★★Friends★Parent/Child

These two signs speak completely different languages. You like to commit to relationships right off the bat. Unconventional Aquarius can't stand being tied down. They like to chat, laugh, discover, and contemplate humanity and the world at large. The only thing you want to contemplate is your cozy surroundings. You just can't understand—*what are they looking for?*

Taurus and Aquarius friends really dislike what drives the other and can only get so close before their differences begin to pop up. Aquarians like to see themselves as nonconformists—you just think they're bizarre. As for parents and children, Aquarians live in their heads, and you live so much in the physical world that there is nothing to connect the two.

Taurus and Pisces:
★★★★Romance ★ ★ ★ Friends ★ ★ ★ Parent/Child

The Bull and the Fish have needs and desires that are perfectly matched to each other. Pisces are emotional and sentimental and shower their sweeties with love letters and affection. You provide them with a safe place to swim—and you love all the attention. You like to be needed, and they are needy. It's perfect!

Taurus and Pisces friendships are worthwhile, but they lack common goals and activities that often unite friends. A Pisces parent understands a Taurus child as not many people can.

GEMINI   AIR   MAY 21–JUNE 20

Gemini and Aries:
★ ★ ★ Romance ★★★★Friends ★ ★ ★ Parent/Child

Lively, chatty, and adventurous, Gemini and Aries are a very good match. The Twins and the Ram love to go to parties—you to meet as many people as you can, and Aries to strut their stuff. You are attracted to Aries' raw energy, but for this to last, look at how they channel it before you get too charmed by first impressions. Geminis need partners to keep their minds active, not just their bodies.

Gemini and Aries friends are both rarely in gloomy moods, so the laughter keeps coming. Here's a tip to make parent/child relations work: If Aries tries to bully you, use your intelligence to sidestep them instead of provoking it more.

Gemini and Taurus:
★Romance★ ★Friends★ ★Parent/Child

From the beginning this relationship doesn't show many signs of life. Serious, stable Taurus can bore the chatty, light Gemini. Gemini's quick pace can make Taurus dizzy. You are interested in people, places, and things. Taureans are interested in home, possessions, and financial stability. Prediction: One conversation and it's over.

Friends of this pairing are a better fit. They can share their interests with each other and expand their horizons—it just won't be a very deep friendship. Taurus parents create stable homes in which Gemini can begin their explorations. Gemini parents move from one activity to another, giving otherwise reserved Taurus a broad taste of experiences.

Gemini and Gemini:
★★★★Romance ★★★★Friends ★★★★Parent/Child

Many same-sign romances don't work because the couple is too much alike—not with two Geminis. The symbol of Gemini is the Twins, and a romance is like being one half of the pair. You're both talkative and curious, with a wide variety of interests and an innate mutual understanding. You give each other the freedom you need and are accepting of each other. The problem: You are both fickle and indecisive, and you fall in and out of love quickly enough without having that influence doubled by two.

Gemini friends, parents, and children work on the same principles. Your relationships are lively, but you both like to keep things so light that there is a danger of never getting below the surface.

Gemini and Cancer:
★ Romance ★ ★ Friends ★ ★ Parent/Child

Gemini and Cancer pairings have about as much a chance of success as a burning fire in Antarctica. Cancers are moody, and one hint of whininess would send you running. You like to be out and about, and you prize freedom. The only place Cancers like to roam is their own neighborhood. The minute you get bored is the minute Cancers are most likely to get clingy. Caution: Don't let the door hit you on the way out.

Friends of this match are a bit easier on each other. Geminis like to have friends in many places, and Cancers keep their friends long after they've outgrown them. Cancer parents should beware of suffocating their Gemini children.

Gemini and Leo:
★★★Romance★★★★Friends★★★Parent/Child

Gemini and Leo make a grand romance. This pairing adds up to a lot of fun, with mutual respect built in for good measure. Gemini's flirtatiousness would have some other signs cringing, but Leo's healthy ego can take it. On a bad day, Leos want more attention and adoration than you want to hand over. That's when your restlessness kicks in and leaves the Lion in an uproar.

These friends are a zodiac success story, just as long as you don't try to outdo each other with your wit and vitality. Relationships between parents and children do well. Gemini kids will naturally give Leo parents their space to roar, and Leos will like not having to compete to be number one.

Gemini and Virgo:
★Romance★ ★Friends★Parent/Child

Gemini and Virgo use their minds in opposite ways, and that's the downfall of this relationship. You are funny, quick-witted, and chatty. Virgos are logical and critical. You use your social skills and outgoing nature to win friends and get ahead in life. Virgos love facts and details, analyzing, reorganizing, and perfecting things. You avoid Virgos' bouts of martyrdom like the plague.

Friends will have enough in common to get by if you don't get too close. Parent/child Gemini/ Virgos will not easily understand each other, but if you try hard, you'll get by.

Gemini and Libra:
★★★★Romance★★★★Friends★★★★Parent/Child

When two air signs meet, they create quite a whirlwind. Your wit, intelligence, and social skills are a perfect match. Since you have so much in common, you'll probably have the same goals and desires in life. You'll have so much to talk about that you'll never get bored, and Libra will play your devil's advocate once in a while—just for the sake of a good argument. The pitfall: You are both indecisive and like the good life. When the two of you are together, this can get a bit out of control.

Friends, parents, and children of the Gemini/ Libra pairing are as perfect together as romantic mates. Just make sure one of you has your feet firmly planted on the ground at all times, so your relationship doesn't get so light that it floats away.

Gemini and Scorpio:
★★Romance★★Friends★★Parent/Child

Gemini and Scorpio pair off for a little while before their opposite natures turn their relationship into a boxing match. Scorpios are forceful and dynamic creatures, and this excites you until you see their possessiveness and jealousy. You are open about who you are. Scorpios are secretive and mysterious. As if that isn't enough, wait until they catch your innocent flirting and accuse you of some devious plot. This won't happen right away, so enjoy the romance while it lasts.

Friendships between Geminis and Scorpios can be quite creative and inspiring if you are both shooting for a common goal. Just don't expect to be compatible in other areas of your life. Parents and children of this pairing can find this relationship rewarding or combustible, depending upon the day of the week.

Gemini and Sagittarius:
★ ★ Romance ★ ★ ★ Friends ★ ★ ★ Parent/Child

Two words describe the relationship between Geminis and Sagittarians: *quick* and *impulsive*. You know: You meet, you flirt, you have a wild time, you see each other every night of the week for a month. At some point you both get restless and want your freedom, and then the flame burns out. It's great fun, but it won't last forever.

Gemini and Sag friends are both thinkers and have so many interests that you're bound to have a few in common. Gemini and Sag parents and children get along famously. You both may feel stifled, but in this relationship it's okay to have your space and eat it too.

Gemini and Capricorn:
★ Romance ★ Friends ★ Parent/Child

If you are thinking about dating a Capricorn, put this book down and take a cold shower. Geminis live a fun and free lifestyle. You like to explore and to live in the moment. Capricorns are all about work. They are cautious and conservative. You spend your time being a social butterfly—Capricorns think that's silly. Geminis talk about a bunch of things, but

Capricorns discuss "serious business." A day of this, and you'd be majorly bored.

Gemini/Capricorn friends can get along for short periods of time if you have a mutual interest that's serious enough for Capricorn and sophisticated enough for Gemini. Parent/child relations are loving, but neither Capricorns nor Geminis are into showing it.

Gemini and Aquarius:
★★★★Romance ★★★★Friends ★★★★Parent/Child

Air sign relationships are amazing! You have so much in common: intelligence, wit, and the love of freedom and travel. You agree on so much that you'll rarely have an argument. This is a good thing, too, since both of you avoid deep emotional conflicts like the plague. One drawback, though, is the inconsistent and unpredictable nature of both your signs. Things may be a bit bumpy until you find a good flow.

Friends in this air sign combination also fit well together, blowing in and out of each other's lives like the wind. Aquarians make the perfect parents for Geminis. They think as fast as you do and understand your need for space and independence.

Gemini and Pisces:
★ Romance ★ ★ Friends ★ Parent/Child

You're full of good ideas, but dating a Pisces isn't one of them. At first it may seem that you have a lot in common—you're both artistic and refined—but that's where it ends. Pisces are emotional, and you avoid raw emotions whenever possible. They're sensitive, mysterious, and needy. You don't understand their slippery depths, and besides, you don't want to go there. You're having too much fun flying around to be dragged into the ocean.

Gemini and Pisces are too different to have a profound friendship. Pisces parents are fickle, changeable, and indecisive, just like Geminis. Let's hope that there is another adult in the house, or nobody will start or finish anything.

CANCER WATER JUNE 21–JULY 22

Cancer and Aries:
★ Romance ★ ★ Friends ★ Parent/Child

Aries is a tough sign to get along with, but for a Cancer, it's nearly impossible. You are a calm, loving homebody, and Aries are spirited adventurers. Ram's energy would agitate you, and your sensitivity would aggravate them further. Your sensitive and sentimental nature is so foreign to them that they would end up hurting your feelings without even realizing it.

Cancer/Aries friendships are short-lived and based on mutual interests, not on a deep mutual understanding. Parents and children of this combination will have a lot of ups and downs. Aries need to be the center of attention, and if you are in one of your famous moods, the last thing you want to do is jump through hoops for them.

Cancer and Taurus:
★★★★Romance ★★★★Friends ★★★★Parent/Child

Wow, what a pair. Crabs and Bulls have so many of the same desires, yet are different enough to keep it interesting. Both of you are warm and passionate, love to stay close to home, and are publicly reserved and conservative with money. To top it off, Taurus are possessive and like attention, and you are clingy and affectionate!

Cancer and Taurus friends think alike and have many of the same hobbies. This friendship has staying power. Parents and children of Cancer and Taurus relate just as well. Cancer's creativity perks up stable Taurus, and Taurus' easygoing style is a positive influence on Cancer's mood swings.

Cancer and Gemini:
★ Romance ★ ★ Friends ★ ★ Parent/Child

Romance between Cancers and Geminis doesn't last much longer than a first date. You talk about your emotions and the things that make you feel secure. They flirt with the waiter and make jokes about the people at the next table. You want to make an emotional connection, but they only want some fun times.

Friends make a better combination. Geminis can talk all they want, and Cancers are good listeners. Parents and children of this match can make it through in one piece if Geminis learn how to handle Cancer's moodiness, and Cancers try not to take everything that comes out of Geminis' chatty mouths personally.

Cancer and Cancer:
★ ★ Romance ★ ★ ★ Friends ★ ★ ★ Parent/Child

You're so much alike in your sensitivity, dependency, and need for security. You can understand each other without saying a word, or you can end up easily hurting each other. The success of this romance is determined by the other aspects of both charts. Your Moon, Venus, and Mars signs will decide whether these similarities are going to make or break this love connection. (See chapter 5, "Beyond the Basics," for that information.)

Cancer friends can read each other's feelings at a glance, but you just can't predict each other's moods. Two Crabs make sensitive, huggy, kissy families, except that both want to hold on to each other for dear life. It's okay to let go!

Cancer and Leo:
★★Romance★★★Friends★★★Parent/Child

Usually a water sign and a fire sign mix like oil and water, but this case is different—how different depends on how much you're both willing to let go of your stuff. Leos are openhearted, cheerful, and generous, and Cancers are attracted to all that energy. Leos love to get attention, and Cancers love to give it. On the other hand, Leos like to take the lead and would scoff at your clingy possessiveness. Leos are much more social than you, and they like to take things a notch bigger than you're comfortable with. Get used to it if you want to stay together.

Lion and Crab can be good friends. Cancerian intuition understands lordly Leo's nature. Cancer and Leo parents and children can have a great deal of fun together. Leo's naturally positive ways can be an upper for Cancer's mood swings.

Cancer and Virgo:
★ ★ ★ Romance ★ ★ ★ Friends ★ ★ ★ Parent/Child

Even though Cancers are emotional and Virgos are logical, this combination does surprisingly well. You both love stability, take relationships seriously, engage in deep conversation, and have a need to protect each other. The negative side of the coin: Virgos aren't emotional enough to handle your moods, and you can take their critical side to heart.

Cancers and Virgos make fine friends. Your similar goals in life build strong bonds. Cancer/Virgo parents and children fulfill each other's needs, creating a solid foundation. Cancer brings creativity to the home, and Virgo brings practicality.

Cancer and Libra:
★ Romance ★ ★ Friends ★ Parent/Child

Cancers and Libras live by two different sets of rules. Cancers like a loving and emotionally secure environment, but Libras search for cerebral elegance. Like all air signs, Libras tend to be emotionally detached. Not getting what you need from a Libra would make you first nervous and then clingy. In response, Libras would find you too testy and smothering.

Cancer and Libra friendships don't have much common ground. Cancers like to socialize with intimate groups, and Libras enjoy meeting and charming large groups of admirers. Parents and children of these two conflict, because Cancers are overprotective and Libras prize their freedom.

Cancer and Scorpio:
★★★★Romance ★★★★Friends ★★★★Parent/Child

These two water signs create great romance and passion together. You both love commitment, dedication, and emotional intimacy. Once you focus on each other, you'll never wander—and that's good, because both of you have quite a jealous streak. Cancers and Scorpios both like to totally possess their mates. Scorpios may go after you more intensely, but all that dynamite makes you hold on tighter—and they love that.

Cancer and Scorpio friends are like two peas in a pod. You are so much alike, you can't get enough of each other. Water sign parents and children share a special depth and understanding. Eruptions and mood swings come as part of the package.

Cancer and Sagittarius:
★Romance★★Friends★Parent/Child

Put a Cancer with a Sag, and you have a bad reaction waiting to happen. Sagittarians are truly independent, but Cancers search for security from those they love. Try as you might, you're not getting it from a Sag. Freedom is an obsession with the Archer, and that just gets your jealous juices flowing. Sagittarian fire can burn your sweet sensitivities. On top of that, as soon as a Sagittarius gets a whiff of one of your less than sunny moods, it'll be over.

You two will be better friends than romantic partners. Your creativity is sparked by their intellectual curiosity—just don't expect them to keep an appointment. Cancer/Sagittarius parent/child relations are cordial. Cancerians love their families, and Sagittarians just love having a good time.

Cancer and Capricorn:
★★Romance★★★Friends★★Parent/Child

This relationship is a toss-up. Located on opposite sides of the zodiac, you have complementary traits. Cancers are loving, emotional, and dependent. Capricorns are the universe's loners, preferring to work rather than play. This can drive you crazy because you might not get your needs met, and Cancers get critical if they are not getting their emotional fix. On the other hand, the security a hardworking Capricorn brings can be quite attractive to you.

Cancer and Capricorn make good friends. Just don't expect the other to be like you. Instead, focus on learning from each other. This combination of parents and children may not understand each other completely, but Cancer's love of home and Capricorn's love of security make a nice mix.

Cancer and Aquarius:
★ Romance ★ ★ Friends ★ ★ Parent/Child

These two are as different as the tortoise and the hare. Original and expressive Aquarius is an intellectual maverick, and that offends Cancer's conservative tastes and cautious disposition. No matter how much you turn on your touchy-feely charm, you can never make that Aquarius quite yours. The more you try, the more they'll resist—and that would make your insecurities more obvious.

Cancer and Aquarius don't pick each other as friends unless you have some common interest or convenience. Crab and Waterbearer parents and children get along best if Cancer tries to appeal to Aquarius' worldly humanitarian qualities, and Aquarius remembers Cancer's sensitivities and moodiness.

Cancer and Pisces:
★★★★Romance ★★★★Friends ★★★★Parent/Child

Cancer and Pisces find themselves in watery paradise. You're both emotional, affectionate, sentimental, compassionate, and intuitive. You both love romance, and your creativity makes this relationship an unforgettable journey. This relationship does have its downside: You're both indecisive, insecure, and prone to mood swings. Most of the time you're well aware of each other's bad days, but you can easily hurt each other if you feel neglected or misunderstood.

These two water signs will enjoy a deep and lasting friendship. They know each other so well, it's as if they mirror each other's souls. Parent/child Cancer/Pisces also have a deep understanding of one another. The only problem is that they can become too dependent on one another.

LEO   FIRE   JULY 23–AUGUST 22

Leo and Aries:
★★★★Romance ★★★★Friends ★★★Parent/Child

Leo and Aries together is a glorious match. When a Leo and an Aries couple walk into a room, you own it. Together you are an unstoppable team. But all that

raw power can get a little scary at times, and any disagreements are bound to be large and loud. Both of
you expect to be the leader. You have a lot of mutual
respect, but neither of you is about to shower the
other with adoration, so you won't get as much as
you're used to.

Friends, parents, and children of this combination
are also tops, just as long as you both recognize that
the relationship isn't a contest.

Leo and Taurus:
★ Romance ★ ★ Friends ★ Parent/Child

These are two of the most obstinate and determined
signs in the zodiac. Pairing off would be a huge mis-
take. You are upbeat and social, and they're quiet and
reserved. You like to be adored, and Taurus likes devotion. There is no way that either of you is going to
give the other that kind of attention. It's a never-
ending downward spiral: The less you get, the more
you demand it. The louder you get, the more stubborn Taurus becomes. Before you know it, you and
the Bull are squaring off in the ring.

These two signs are so willful that the friendships
don't do much better, but at least friends don't have
to live together. Parent/child Leo and Taurus combinations work best if you learn the meaning of the
word *compromise*!

Leo and Gemini:
★★★Romance★★★★Friends★★★Parent/Child

Leos and Geminis have a lot in common. Both are fun, theatrical types, outgoing and personable, each in their own way—Leos because they're the commanders of the zodiac, and Geminis because they're the communicators. This relationship is filled with spontaneity and adventure. The only problem is that you like to be catered to, and sometimes your Gemini is off exploring their independence. When you don't get the adoration you expect, things can get a little dicey.

Leo and Gemini friends are popular and social. They don't belong to a specific clique, but would much rather be welcomed by large groups of friends and admirers. This is a supportive and fun relationship between parent and child as well. Don't try to hold on to your Gemini, and don't demand too much gratitude in return for giving them what they want.

Leo and Cancer:
★★Romance★★★Friends★★★Parent/Child

Leos and Cancers are passionate people, and you're both expressive in different ways—Leos because you're flamboyant, and Cancers because of their neediness. When you invite a Crab into your life, they'll shower you with love and affection, and want to hold on to you forever. You love all the attention—that is, as long as your Cancer doesn't get too clingy. It's true that Leos are social and Cancers are homebodies, but if you can compromise on the energy level, you've got something worth working at.

Leos and Cancers make good friends, too. Cancers are attracted to all that energy and will gladly follow your lead, unless they're in one of their gloomy moods and don't feel like it. Parents and children match up. Both take an interest in a positive home life—Cancers for the love of family, and Leos for the attention.

Leo and Leo:
★★Romance★★Friends★★Parent/Child

Two Leos together have quite a commanding presence. You both are regal, refined, and extravagant. During good times you inspire each other to be even bigger. During bad times, you compete to run the show. After all, unless your world is big enough for two rulers, you're bound to have clashes. This can be a fabulous match, but with two egos like yours, the chances of this lasting forever are slim.

Leo friends burn hot, and that can be both good and bad—but never boring. Parent/child Lions have so much energy that it can be overwhelming. Look out when the child goes through adolescence!

Leo and Virgo:
★Romance★★Friends★Parent/Child

Leos are dramatic and theatrical, and Virgos are sensible and realistic. Leos think very highly of themselves, and Virgos are extremely critical. Virgos are like sandpaper to your ego—not good. You live for the big picture, Virgos for the details. The bottom line: If you were on a date you'd be at each other's throats before the the main course was served.

Leo and Virgo friends get along better. Virgos can organize Leos' passions—just don't expect them to adore you. Leo/Virgo parent/child relationships are about as good as spoiled milk. Leos are full of love, and Virgos are all about stability, but over time Leos don't get enough of what they need in return and can get ornery.

Leo and Libra:
★★★Romance★★★★Friends★★★Parent/Child

A classic prideful Leo and a refined, social Libra deserve two stars, but more often than not, aspects such as the sign of the Moon, Mars, and Venus play a big role in softening the classic character traits (see chapter 5, "Beyond the Basics," for details). It comes down to this: You're both extravagant and like nice things. You're more passionate, Libras more cerebral. Libra weighs the issues, and you just like the issues to come out in your favor. Libras play devil's advocate and can be quite adamant about it—that would have you in an uproar.

Friends of this combination work well if they can share the spotlight. Parents and children of this matching will do a lot of fun and creative things together. The playground is the stage for their show.

Leo and Scorpio:
★Romance★ ★Friends★ ★Parent/Child

Leos and Scorpios have the same energy and passion, but that's all you have in common. Scorpio's passions are intense and deep, while Leo's are generous and extravagant. Leo's active social life has Scorpio on high alert. Scorpios have a way of suspecting the worst, never quite trusting your wild activities. The next thing you know, suspicious Scorpio is making a scene. They're way too temperamental for your cheery disposition—and they'd never give you the constant attention you deserve.

Leo and Scorpios can work better as friends than as a romantic couple, because you're attracted to each other's spirited energy. Leo and Scorpio family relations will be loving but explosive.

Leo and Sagittarius:
★★★★Romance ★★★★Friends ★★★★Parent/Child

Leo and Sagittarius both have an exuberant, fiery nature. You're both adventurous, independent, and good-natured. You're active socially—Sagittarians like to explore new people, and Leos like to gather more admirers. Leos like to take control, and Sags hate responsibility—this match is perfect. The downfall: Lead them you may, but try to dominate them and they're out of here.

Leo and Sagittarius make for a spirited and life-affirming friendship. Other people want to get to know these two. Leo and Sagittarius parents and children have a supportive relationship, as long as the Archer's need for freedom doesn't leave the Lion feeling ignored.

Leo and Capricorn:
★Romance★Friends★★Parent/Child

Sorry, this romantic pairing is the worst possible! Leos are bright and sunny, and like to be followed around by a lively group of friends. Capricorns are practical workaholics who much prefer getting stuff done to aimless socializing. Capricorns are critical of your extravagance and emotionally lack the expressiveness you need to feel appreciated.

These two can be friends if Leo is directing a huge production and needs someone to organize it, but your Capricorn isn't going to hang around for long—there are too many things to do. Parent/child Leos/Capricorns don't do much for each other. Leos will try to lighten up Capricorn's serious outlook, but don't expect success.

Leo and Aquarius:
★★Romance★★★Friends★★Parent/Child

Leos and Aquarians are both opinionated and set in their ways. Yes, you have an initial attraction, but can you sustain this past the dating stage? You're both creative, energetic, and social, but Aquarians will be irked by all the attention going your way. Share the spotlight and you have a chance.

This combination works much better as friends. You can socialize all you want and get your emotional needs met elsewhere. Parent/child Leo/Aquarius pairs can be a success with some effort. Aquarians need to back away from analyzing everything, and Leos need to compromise their command.

Leo and Pisces:
★Romance★★Friends★Parent/Child

Lordly Leo and otherworldly Pisces are a complete mismatch. They're both creative, and that can get them through a couple of dates, but the exuberant Lion tramples Pisces' emotional sensitivities. You love being out and about, making new friends and mastering new experiences. The only things quiet Pisces want to master is their connection with the universe. It's true that they're loving and demonstrative and you can never get enough attention, but their tendency to withdraw would drive you bonkers.

Leo and Pisces are better suited as friends when your creative energies can come out and play. Then you can go home before your tolerance for each other hits low levels. Parents and children of this pairing will have a rough time unless Pisces can learn to set boundaries and not take everything so personally.

Virgo   Earth
August 23–September 22

Virgo and Aries:
★ *Romance* ★ ★ *Friends* ★ *Parent/Child*

Virgos and Aries don't play for the same team. You're quiet, practical perfectionists, and Aries are raucous rabble-rousers. You think, and they act. You work, and they play. You look down at their attempts to dominate you, and your desire to perfect them aggravates them. They don't want to be all they can be—they think too highly of themselves already.

Virgo and Aries friends have a better chance of success, because the world needs both activators and organizers. Parents and children of this pairing will have problems communicating. Virgo-talk is sensible and analytic, but Aries-speak is abrupt, energetic, and emotional.

Virgo and Taurus:
★★★★Romance★ ★ ★ Friends★ ★ ★ Parent/Child

These two earth signs are perfect together. Both are practical, hardworking providers who love to create a safe environment for themselves and their mates. You usually keep your emotions in a secure place, and Taureans are great at bringing them out in the open. Quiet, cautious, and efficient, you're so much alike that it could be your downfall. Romance and excitement aren't your top priorities.

Friendships between Virgo and Taurus are strong, and they're based on similar expectations of life and each other. Parent/child Virgo/Taurus pairs are safe and stable. You need to keep an eye on your criticism, and Taureans need to watch their stubbornness.

Virgo and Gemini:
★Romance★ ★Friends★ Parent/Child

The only thing Virgos and Geminis are good for is getting on each other's nerves. You both do a lot of talking and thinking, but your minds work so differently that they never meet. Geminis are impulsive, airy, and adaptable. You're grounded, discriminating, and reserved. Geminis love their freedom and are always searching for new experiences. You value stability and always seek to analyze and perfect everything. Geminis resent you for trying to change them, and you resent them for not sticking around long enough to work things out.

Virgos and Geminis can be friends. Just don't expect them to be your *best* friend—you're too different. Virgo/Gemini parents and children are also so different that they have a hard time understanding one another.

Virgo and Cancer:
★ ★ ★Romance★ ★ ★ ★Friends★ ★ ★ Parent/Child

Your down-to-earth style complements this water sign well. Both Virgos and Cancers strive for security. Cancers are affectionate, possessive, and dependent. All that devotion makes you feel needed. You like Cancer's energy level, and their emotional nature brings out your hidden passions. Watch out for the Crab's infamous mood swings—no one is immune to them. Be forewarned: Both Virgos and Cancers are way too critical.

Virgo and Cancer friends hit it off in a major way. You both value privacy and are good at keeping secrets. Parent/child relations are supportive, although Cancers have a tendency to smother their children. That's okay; you just don't care to be demonstrative yourself.

Virgo and Leo:
★ Romance ★ ★ Friends ★ Parent/Child

You have a better chance of winning the lottery than you do of having a successful relationship with a Leo. First of all, Leos come on too strong, and you hate that. Leos have big egos and big wallets. You're dignified and practical with money. They love to be showered with admiration, and you have better things to do than to flatter a Lion with empty praise. To top it off, you're a perfectionist. You'll try to fix your Leo—and they just don't want to go there.

Virgos and Leos don't have enough in common to sustain a deep and lasting friendship, but if you're thrown together, you'll like each other enough to get by. If they don't watch out, parent/child Virgo/Leo pairs can look down on each other's style and get on each other's nerves.

Virgo and Virgo:
★★Romance★★★Friends★★★Parent/Child

There are worse pairings than two Virgos, but there are better ones, too. You think alike and understand each other very well, but too many similarities may not be good for romance. You'd create a stable relationship, be sensitive to each other's needs, and revel in doing things for each other. When you turn your perfectionist leanings against each other, though, you can be critical and nitpicky and can get easily hurt.

Two Virgo friends will have that same deep understanding and will always feel safe and secure within the friendship. There are positives and negatives to parent/child Virgos. Living in a perfectionist's house can make you feel insecure, but you will be taught to develop the skills that suit you best.

Virgo and Libra:
★Romance★★Friends★Parent/Child

You can tell by the number of stars that this relationship isn't worth it. Virgos take love much more seriously than their Libra counterparts. Libras love to socialize, spend money, and look good for a living.

You are much too practical and hardworking for that. Picture-perfect Virgos are too detail-oriented for Libras; what you look at as perfecting, they see as abrasive. Also, Virgos try to step in and take control when Libras get wishy-washy, and that sends their scales out of balance.

Virgo and Libra friendships flow more smoothly, because Virgos aren't as critical of acquaintances as they are in romantic relationships, and Libras' social skills put Virgos at ease. Virgo/Libra parent/child relationships can be emotionally lacking. Virgos are known for their reserve and Libras for their detachment.

Virgo and Scorpio:
★ ★ ★ Romance ★ ★ ★ ★ Friends ★ ★ Parent/Child

You might think that a reserved Virgo and an intense Scorpio wouldn't get along—but that's not true. Scorpios' energy may take some getting used to, but their possessiveness makes Virgos feel safe. You're such a private person, but you can't hide anything from Scorpio's piercing eyes. The pitfall: You're both controlling. Work that out to achieve harmony.

Virgos and Scorpios make intelligent, perceptive friends, and admire those qualities in each other. Virgo/Scorpio parents and children work well for the most part. Sometimes Scorpios can come on too strong for subdued Virgos, and they both have bite. Virgos are critical, and Scorpios are volatile and brooding.

Virgo and Sagittarius:
★ Romance ★ Friends ★ Parent/Child

No way will a Virgo last more than a minute with a Sagittarius. They're freewheeling, fun-loving risk takers. Conservative Virgos look at them as reckless. You just can't understand why they wouldn't want to be more responsible. If you try to get them to change their wanton ways, you quickly discover that there is no way you can control or sedate a Sagittarius.

Virgo and Sagittarius can be friends, but would often find it difficult to hang out together. Virgo/Sag parents and children have to struggle to get along. Virgos like order and precision, but Sagittarians are spontaneous and indulgent. You make sure everything is in its proper place, and Sagittarians mess things up.

Virgo and Capricorn:
★★★★Romance ★★★★Friends ★★★★Parent/Child

These two earth signs are made for each other. You are both hardworking overachievers who count stability and security among your highest priorities. If you bring that dedication into your relationship, it will be easy for each of you to please the other. The weaknesses: Neither of you is comfortable sharing your deep feelings and emotions. You both take things personally, get easily hurt, and then hold it in—not good.

Virgo and Capricorn friendships are grounded in reality and can last a lifetime. Parents and children will have an easy time relating, except for the fact that you're both so realistic. Make sure you have some fun creative time, too.

Virgo and Aquarius:
★Romance★ ★Friends★ ★Parent/Child

These signs are too different to make a go of it successfully. Aquarians are progressive and unorthodox, whereas Virgos are cautious and conservative. You weigh all the risks before taking the most practical path, and Aquarians are so independent that they'll take the risky road just to be different. Achieving personal goals is the way you achieve success. Aquarians measure success on a more global and humanitarian scale.

Relationships between friends, or between parents and children, have a bigger chance of making it, because Virgos like to serve others and Aquarians are friendly and social.

Virgo and Pisces:
★★Romance★★★Friends★★★Parent/Child

A Virgo and a Pisces make a pretty good match. You're pretty compatible but have some conflicting traits. To a romantic, affectionate, and dependent Pisces, love is everything. Their qualities make Virgos feel confident. Also, Virgos love to be indispensable, and Pisces folk can be a bit needy and fragile sometimes. But Pisces are dreamy procrastinators, and Virgos are practical doers. If you spend enough time with one, you might haul out that critical nature of yours and let that Pisces have it.

Virgo and Pisces are naturally drawn to each other. Virgos can add practicality to Piscean creativity, and Pisces are all too happy to let Virgos organize. Parent/child Virgo/Pisces pairs can hit some rough patches every once in a while, but you're caring people.

LIBRA   AIR
SEPTEMBER 23–OCTOBER 22

Libra and Aries:
★★Romance★★★Friends★★★Parent/Child

An undeniable attraction exists between Libras and Aries. You're opposites on the zodiac's pie chart (see

p. 4), which is a good thing. You admire Aries' zest for life and their outgoing nature. Aries can take you out in style. On the other hand, you turn your nose up at Aries' impulsiveness. Aries love their independence, but enjoy committing to a partner. You'd rather date awhile before making a decision that big, and the Ram just doesn't have that kind of patience.

Friendships and parent/child relationships fare better. If you learn to love and accept Aries' sometimes brash ways, they'll be very loyal to you.

Libra and Taurus:
★★Romance★★★Friends★★Parent/Child

Libra and Taurus share their ruling planet: Venus. That makes you artistic and attracted to beautiful things. You both like to collect these objects of beauty, but while Taureans have one eye on the object and one eye on the price, you know that you deserve what you want, whatever the cost. Although both of you are easygoing, Taureans are slow and methodical, and you are much more lively. Also, the Bull likes to stay at home, and you'd much rather be out on the town with your friends.

Libra and Taurus will be better friends. Just don't try to tell Taureans what to do, or you'll see their famous stubborn streak. Taurean parents get a bit obstinate, but you can get pretty opinionated yourself.

Libra and Gemini:
★★★★Romance ★★★★Friends ★★★Parent/Child

This is one of the universe's perfect pairings. Both are light, social, and artistic. When these two come together, the fun never stops. You both thrive on change and excitement, intellectual curiosity, and a wide variety of social engagements. You also hate any kind of possessiveness, boredom, and deep emotional conflicts. You're both fickle and indecisive. You can never figure out exactly what you want out of the relationship.

Friend and parent/child relationships of this pairing are also bright. You can be assured that your friendship will be one big splash after another. The only downfall in parent/child relations is that there is little emotional sensitivity, and neither one of you particularly like to get down to the nitty-gritty. If you're lucky, you have a water, earth, or fire sign around to bring in a little balance.

Libra and Cancer:
★ Romance★ ★ Friends★ Parent/Child

If you meet a Cancer, whatever you do, don't ask them out. You're social and genuinely interested in people, but Cancers are cautious and private. They're savers, but you like to spend. When you're out eating at the hottest new restaurant in town, they're cooking in the comfort of their home. Crabs need affection to feel loved, and you just need physical attraction and good conversation.

Friends of this pairing work better. They're great listeners, and you're great talkers, but they like to talk about deep emotional issues, and you like to talk about yourself! Libra/Cancer parents and children don't get each other. They're emotional, and you are cerebral.

Libra and Leo:
★ ★ ★ Romance ★ ★ ★ ★ Friends ★ ★ ★ Parent/Child

Pleasure-loving Libra and extravagant Leo are a very good match. You're both lively, social, and love to spend money. Ego is the downside of this relationship. Leos have plenty of it, and sometimes you want your share of the attention. You argue for argument's sake, and Leos like to argue to get their way. Always be armed with grace and tact if you plan to keep this romance going.

Libra and Leo make the best of friends. Their generous and fun-loving outlook makes them popular party guests. Libra and Leo parents and children mostly get along very well. They will always have to be on their best behavior to share the spotlight, though. Leos can get domineering and angry when they're crossed, and Libras' tenaciousness can just add insult to injury.

Libra and Virgo:
★Romance★★Friends★Parent/Child

Virgos have an understated charm that attracts Libra—but not for long. You will soon find out that practical and prudent Virgos dislike your social, pleasure-seeking ways. You look at their quiet, stay-at-home sensibilities and think: *Boring!* They look at your lavish tastes and think: *Frivolous!* The nail in the coffin is their detail-oriented nit-picking. The only way you can avoid criticism from a Virgo is to leave.

Friendships between Libras and Virgos are less frightening. You're both intelligent and analytical, and enjoy a good conversation. Parent/child Libra/Virgos will not have it easy. Virgos are hard-working perfectionists, and Libras want to get away with as little work as possible.

Libra and Libra:
★★Romance★★★Friends★★★Parent/Child

Two Libras in one relationship can be hit or miss. On a good day, you're both charming, social people-pleasers who love to spend money. On a bad day, you're frivolous with love and emotionally checked out. You both like to flirt, and you're always into doing new things. This can be either good or bad—you choose.

Two indecisive Libra friends are all talk, little action. Two Scales make for a lot of wavering. Parent and child Libras enjoy pleasing each other. You also like to have a good debate. You choose sides, not because you feel strongly about a subject, but because you enjoy the opposition.

Libra and Scorpio:
★ Romance ★ Friends ★ Parent/Child

Scorpio's watery intensity dampens your airy style. You are flirty, easygoing, and diplomatic—and Scorpios are anything but. They are possessive, secretive, strong-willed, and moody. They want to know where you're going and where you've been since the minute they last laid eyes on you. They insist on three things casual Libras loathe: commitment, unfaltering loyalty, and emotional dependency.

For a friendship of this match to work, you will have to be the accommodating one, since Scorpios aren't able to turn down the heat. Relationships between parent/child Libra/Scorpios require constant adjusting. You thrive on balance and intellectual clarity. They thrive on impulse and eruption.

Libra and Sagittarius:
★★★★Romance ★★★★Friends ★★★★Parent/Child

Libra and Sagittarius add up to the flirtiest relationship in the universe. You're both charming, romantic, and fun-loving. Sagittarians are famous for their freedom-seeking lifestyle. Your light approach to love and similar social interests gives them just what they need. Archers work on instinct, move quickly, and change their minds a lot. You are more intellectual, weigh all the facts, and waffle on your decisions. Also, both of you are pretty anticommitment. In fact, some Sagittarians are commitment-phobic.

Libra/Sagittarius friends rate high for compatibility even though Sagittarians are more adventuresome and Libras are more refined and diplomatic. Parents and children of this combination get along well naturally, although they may try to get you to take more risks.

Libra and Capricorn:
★ Romance ★ Friends ★ Parent/Child

Capricorns are beneath your elegant sensibilities. You may be able to charm them in the beginning, but you'll soon get the Capricorn cold shoulder. It's not that Capricorns are unfriendly, it's just that they're most concerned with success and stability. They don't waste their time chitchatting, and that's one of the things you do best. They are workaholics, and that's just not your thing.

Libras and Capricorns can be friends. Just don't expect them to have a lot of time for you outside their full schedule of meaningful activities. Scale/Goat parent/child relations will be remote. Neither of you is good at sharing your feelings and emotions unless you have another, more demonstrative sign in the house to pry it out of you.

Libra and Aquarius:
★★★★Romance★★★★Friends★★★★Parent/Child

Libras and Aquarians have a deep affinity for each other. You're both intelligent, witty, artistic, and people-oriented. Libras' refined sensibilities go well with Aquarian style and flair. Aquarians are energetic, quick-minded, and decisive. The wishy-washy Scale is thrilled to have someone making decisions who understands you so well. You both have the same innate airy disposition: free, cerebral, unemotional, and fun.

Libra and Aquarius make superb friends. Your similarities make you extremely compatible. Parent/child relationships between these two air signs are entertaining and intellectually stimulating.

Libra and Pisces:
★ ★ Romance ★ ★ Friends ★ ★ Parent/Child

Libra and Pisces are both artistic and affectionate people. Your fondness for romance will get this dalliance off to a good start. But sometime after the real relationship begins, it will start to unravel. You will quickly discover that Pisces are emotionally sensitive and needy. You don't want someone hanging on to you for dear life. This will get worse the more fun and flirty you get. Soon your delicate Pisces will begin to feel neglected and get all whiny. That is when you will say good-bye to the Fish!

Libra and Pisces friends care for each other as long as you get to create your own beautiful world and not have harsh reality rear its ugly head. With Libra/Pisces parents and children the relationship may not be as intimate as Pisces wants, and it may be more emotionally restrictive than you're comfortable with.

SCORPIO   WATER
OCTOBER 23–NOVEMBER 21

Scorpio and Aries:
★ Romance ★ ★ Friends ★ Parent/Child

Scorpio and Aries are like two cars playing chicken: When two such powerful signs get together, the thing they're best at creating is explosions. Aries' power is open, free, flirty, and domineering. Scorpio's power is deep, secretive, possessive, and controlling. This relationship is going to come down to one thing: who gets to win.

Scorpio and Aries are both creative and energetic. They'll be happy friends as long as they hang out in a large pack. Scorpio/Aries parents and children will constantly collide. Both are independent, and neither likes to back down.

Scorpio and Taurus:
★★Romance★★★Friends★★Parent/Child

Scorpio and Taurus both have strong personalities. This relationship potential comes down to how you both handle your obstinate, possessive, and jealous traits. You're emotionally intense, and Taureans are physically intense. You're both thrilled to be smothered by each other until you feel your dominance is being challenged, and then—*boom!* Other people should watch out.

Scorpio and Taurus friendships can be very positive, just as long as you realize you don't own each other. Familial relations experience many highs and lows. They fight, but their love is strong and deep.

Scorpio and Gemini:
★★Romance★★Friends★★Parent/Child

A relationship between these two may not survive a lifetime, but it will be fun while it lasts. Scorpios are attracted to Geminis' intelligence, and Geminis are charmed by your intensity. You like to completely own your partners emotionally, and this is where Geminis get squeamish. They're not fond of emotions to begin with, and they love their freedom too much to give it up for you.

Scorpio and Gemini friendships are full of on-and-off short bursts, Scorpio being responsible for the short bursts and Gemini for the on-and-off. Scorpio/Gemini parents and children understand each other well. You're better at communicating emotions, and Geminis are better at communicating about everything else.

Scorpio and Cancer:
★★★★Romance★★★★Friends★★★★Parent/Child

The romance between these two water signs is rewarding—it just won't always be easy. You both enjoy deep emotional commitments. Cancers are usually withdrawn, but they feel safe to explore in the presence of the powerful Scorpio—and you love all the affection. Both of you are moody and jealous.

You'll understand each other's watery moods, but Scorpio will always come out the dominant one, since Cancers are too cautious.

Water sign friends understand each other as if you have the same essence. Parent/child relations share this same characteristic, although parents can be overprotective and children can easily get lost in their own moods.

Scorpio and Leo:
★Romance★ ★Friends★ ★Parent/Child

If there were a movie about a Scorpio/Leo romance, it would be called *Clash of the Egos*! It would go something like this: Two powerful signs meet and have a great time for a date or two. Then the exuberant Leo begins some normal everyday flirting. The Scorpio gets wildly jealous and demands all the attention. Leo gets loud and angry. Things start flying. The end.

Scorpio and Leo can be friends if your extra energy is being used constructively on a hobby or project. Parents and children of this unruly pairing will have a stormy household unless one of them wants to compromise the need to dominate.

Scorpio and Virgo:
★ ★ ★ Romance ★ ★ ★ Friends ★ ★ Parent/Child

If you're expecting someone exactly like you, then don't go out with a Virgo. If you want a tried-and-true relationship, the Virgo is for you. Yes, Virgos are reserved, but you bring out the best in them. Both of you love to put all of your time and energy into one person. The negatives: They're critical and are prone to indulge in self-pity. You're too spontaneous and have a short fuse.

This match makes great friends, because Virgos like to serve, and Scorpios like to be served. Parents and children of this combination may not be so lucky. A Virgo parent will overplan the Scorpio child's life.

Scorpio and Libra:
★ Romance ★ Friends ★ Parent/Child

This match is just too different to work. Scorpios love to make deep emotional commitments to their significant other, and Libras like to keep things on an intellectual level. The Scale's attitude toward love comes across as too casual for you. No matter how much you try to grab them, they'll always seem elusive to you—and that's not healthy for your ego.

It's not that Scorpio and Libra friends can't get along, it's that they have nothing in common. Scorpios are secretive and intense, Libras light and outgoing. Parent/child Scorpio/Libra pairs don't have an easy time of it. Your deep emotions can upset Libras' cool balance, and they like to pick arguments with you just to watch you get annoyed.

Scorpio and Scorpio:
★★Romance★★Friends★★Parent/Child

Two Scorpios together can be quite a team, but your negative traits can add up to self-destruction. Your emotional depth and sensitivity allow you to understand each other well if your suspicious nature doesn't get the best of you. You're both creative and intense, so you'll never be at a loss for fun and excitement. The bad stuff: You're both jealous, moody, and domineering. Who's going to control the relationship may be your biggest topic of conversation.

Scorpio friends are strongly attracted to each other or strongly repelled by each other—or both. Families with two Scorpios are a loving, intense, and emotional tribe.

Scorpio and Sagittarius:
★Romance★★Friends★Parent/Child

This isn't worth your time and energy. Scorpios like to be involved in deep, gratifying relationships, and

Sagittarians are too busy enjoying their freedom and adventure to stay still for very long. You're private, brooding, and distrustful, and you find them too happy-go-lucky, talkative, and energetic. You can't take their flighty attitude for very long before you want to kick them in the pants.

Scorpio and Sagittarians have enough in common to be friends. You like to be the dominant one, and even though Sags aren't the most consistent friends, they don't mind being second. Parents and children of this pairing will have obstacles. You're extremely over-protective, and Sagittarians are extreme risk takers.

Scorpio and Capricorn:
★ ★ ★ Romance ★ ★ ★ ★ Friends ★ ★ Parent/Child

Volatile Scorpio and steadfast Capricorn make a great romance. All of your overpowering energy focused on the Goat brings them out of their shell. Other signs dislike your jealous possessiveness, but Capricorns love feeling so needed. Unfortunately, they just don't like to show it. You may resent it when your emotional intensity isn't returned by the staid Capricorn. They don't mind your moods as much as you mind theirs.

Both Capricorns and Scorpios are loyal, but don't expect your Capricorn friends to be around if they have work to do. Parent/child relationships between these two signs are supportive, but you want to have your way all the time, and Capricorns are too determined to give it to you.

Scorpio and Aquarius:
★Romance★ ★Friends★ ★Parent/Child

Scorpios and Aquarians don't get along very well. Their airy temperament will irritate you from the beginning. You like to wrap yourselves around your other half and get to know the deepest parts of their soul. Aquarians' freedom-loving, unemotional style will make that impossible. Never knowing where you stand or how important you are to them can make you moody, and they don't do moody. The more they run, the more you try to hold on.

Scorpio and Aquarius make better friends. You're less likely to try to possess and dominate friends to the same degree as you do soul mates. Aquarian parents may not always know how to handle your emotional intensity.

Scorpio and Pisces:
★★★★Romance★★★★Friends★★★★Parent/Child

Profoundly emotional, Scorpio and Pisces is a match made in the depths of the abyss. Both are sensitive, but Pisces' vulnerability brings out your strong, intense character—and Pisces doesn't shy away from that intensity. Instead, Pisces finds it comforting. When Pisces gets needy, Scorpio steps into action. Your overprotective nature is exactly what Pisces needs, and your jealousy is flattering to them.

Scorpio and Pisces make perfect friends. Pisces can create a safe little world for both of them, and you can defend it. Two water sign parents and children understand each other very well. There's likely to be sulking and moodiness, but that doesn't bother either one of you.

SAGITTARIUS FIRE
NOVEMBER 22–DECEMBER 21

Sagittarius and Aries:
★★★★Romance ★★★★Friends ★★★★Parent/Child

These two fire signs are an ideal match! You're both passionate, optimistic, and extreme. You both love traveling, gambling, playing sports, and exploring the great outdoors. You're definitely the more reckless of the two, but Aries understands where you're coming from. Sure, there'll be arguments ahead, but neither of you minds—that's part of your shared fire sign nature.

Sagittarius and Aries friends are physically and

mentally matched. You have the same interests and can talk about them for hours. It's great when family members share the same element. It's easy for them to understand and support each other.

Sagittarius and Taurus:
★ Romance ★ Friends ★ Parent/Child

Taureans are rather slow-moving and serious people. There's no way that a spontaneous and happy-go-lucky Sagittarian can stand such heaviness for a nanosecond. You love adventure, and they love staying home. Try to get them out and about with you and you will soon run into their bullish stubbornness. They also love to hold on to things. How long, do you think, before you flee?

Friends of this pairing are too opposite to share very much. You'd be more willing to give it a try, but Taureans like to have their way too much. Sag and Taurus parents and children have the same problems. With a Taurus parent, you're not likely to get your freedom and autonomy.

Sagittarius and Gemini:
★ ★ Romance ★ ★ ★ Friends ★ ★ ★ Parent/Child

These two are complementary opposites on the zodiac wheel (see p. 4). Sagittarius and Gemini have an

131

initial attraction, but their too-different characteristics may make this hard to sustain. You're both spirited adventure seekers, and your biggest problem is that both of you are wary of commitment. The fling would be fun, but with no foundation, you're just as likely to fly away as you are to stay together.

Friends, and parents and children, of these signs have a much easier time—friends because you can keep coming and going as you please, and family because love will be the glue to make this stick.

Sagittarius and Cancer:
★ Romance ★ ★ Friends ★ Parent/Child

The two of you intrigue each other, but there are more problems than solutions here. You see love as a fun exploration. They like it to be an intimate and dependent union. You want a chatty, responsive, and energetic partner. They want an understated, emotional homebody. You'd always be doing a fast dance through their clingy grasp. One day you'd dance your way out and never look back!

Sagittarius and Cancer friends do better. Cancers will lend an ear to anyone, and Sagittarians are one of the most friendly signs in the zodiac. Parents and children with such opposite natures feel misunderstood, unless they are always aware of each other's needs.

Sagittarius and Leo:
★★★★Romance ★★★★Friends ★★★★Parent/Child

Confident Leo and adventuresome Sagittarius make quite a pair. You both have problems with signs that try to hold you down. Leos are comfortable with themselves and value their own freedom, so you'll never have that problem on this date. You have so much in common with this sign that you won't even realize how much time is flying by and how much you have committed yourself. This relationship can last a millennium!

Two fire signs make fast friends. Follow Leos around and you'll never know the meaning of boredom. Sagittarius and Leo parents and children are always on one big adventure after another. Remember to slow down. Rest and relaxation are not a bad idea once in a while.

Sagittarius and Virgo:
★Romance ★Friends ★Parent/Child

These two get on each other's nerves more than any other pair. Virgos are quiet, cautious, and conservative. Sagittarians are friendly, easygoing, and extravagant. They try to get you to calm down and act more responsibly, and you try to get them to take it easy and have more fun. This drives you both crazy.

Aside from some good conversation, this relationship is going nowhere.

Sagittarius and Virgo friendships work on these same principles. In small doses, this relationship can stay alive. Parents and children of this combination are sure to have problems. Try to be more understanding of each other's nature.

Sagittarius and Libra:
★★★★Romance ★★★★Friends ★★★★Parent/Child

A romance between a Sagittarius and a Libra is a real charmer. Libras are elegant, artistic, and easygoing. As the zodiac's flirt, you love their refined and cerebral nature. You are prone to feeling more restriction than Libras, but they will by no means crowd you—and you'll inspire them to be more adventurous. A warning: They're not always charming. Sometimes they like to pick a good fight.

Sag and Libra friendships are spontaneous and intellectually stimulating. Sagittarius and Libra parents and children will have a close and enjoyable relationship. There might be some challenges, but you're up for it.

To Be or Not to Be

Sagittarius and Scorpio:
★ Romance ★ ★ Friends ★ Parent/Child

Think very carefully before embarking on a Scorpio romance. You may be attracted to their energy, but you just want to explore it and move on. When a Scorpio sets his eyes on you, he wants to delve deep into your psyche, and that is way too intense for your emotional claustrophobia. They're dominating, moody, and jealous—traits that are so against your nature, you'll be changing course in no time.

Friends of this match get along a bit better. Sagittarians are outgoing and nonjudgmental, so you're more willing to accept people, faults and all. Family Sagittarius and Scorpio pairings should watch out. Scorpio's moods and overprotectiveness can make the elusive Sagittarian feel trapped and stifled.

Sagittarius and Sagittarius:
★ ★ Romance ★ ★ ★ Friends ★ ★ ★ Parent/Child

Two Sagittarians have a fabulous romance, while it lasts. Both generous, energetic, and social, you'll have a very giving relationship. You'll make life one big adventure, with tons of spontaneous trips and activities. You're both clever and like to think you know it all, so the arguments should be eventful as well. The biggest problems, though, are your need for freedom, your short attention span for love, and your actions, which border on recklessness. Don't worry—you'll be friends till the end.

Two Sag friends have so much in common. Flirty, fun, and free, they'll attract the same spotlight, but there'll be room enough for two. Sagittarian parents and children totally understand each other's needs for freedom and activity. What a great match!

Sagittarius and Capricorn:
★ Romance ★ ★ Friends ★ Parent/Child

Stick a Sagittarius and a Capricorn in a small room for a day and they're at each other's throats within a matter of hours. There's nothing about one that interests the other—rather, everything repels. You love freedom, spontaneity, flirting, action. They love work above all else, and they are cautious, serious, and cunning. Your extravagance bothers them. They are tightfisted, which bothers you. Better to be friends.

A Sagittarian and a Capricorn can make it as friends because you don't spend a whole lot of time together. You love your freedom, and they love their projects. Parent/child relationships of this pairing have opposite demeanors, and neither of you particularly likes to roll over for anyone.

Sagittarius and Aquarius:
★★★★Romance★★★★Friends★★★★Parent/Child

Sagittarians and Aquarians are made for each other. You are both freedom lovers, social, and active. You are both thinkers and explorers. Date an Aquarius and you'll have everything you want in a mate: a free-thinking, well-bred, intelligent, eccentric, no-holds-barred humanitarian. If any pair can sustain life on the edge, it's you two.

Friends and family members of this coupling will find life a fun-filled, creative adventure, adapting to many new situations and never staying in one place for very long.

Sagittarius and Pisces:
★Romance★★Friends★★Parent/Child

Unless you are willing to sacrifice yourself to the gods, don't commit to a Pisces. Besides some sexy kissing, there's nothing you really like about them. They're dreamy, sensitive, and emotionally dependent. Your need for independence will threaten their fragile balance. They'll want to lean on you 24/7—that will last about a week before you're off exploring life with some other hottie.

Sag and Pisces friends match up a bit better. You're both creative and may find yourselves working together in the same industry. Sagittarius and Pisces parents and children will alternate between being stifling and supportive.

CAPRICORN   EARTH
DECEMBER 22–JANUARY 19

Capricorn and Aries:
★Romance★ ★Friends★Parent/Child

If you want to throw away everything that is important to your well-being, date an Aries. You strive to create security and success in your life, and are very careful to choose your goals and take only the steps you deem worthy. Aries are all over the place—impulsive, gregarious, and domineering. Their main goal is to be the center of attention.

Capricorn and Aries friends have a better chance, because when you have a common goal, you set out to accomplish it with confidence. Familial relations can suffer because of all the head butting going on—that would tire out anyone.

Capricorn and Taurus:
★★★★Romance★★★★Friends★★★★Parent/Child

Home, home on the range. When a Capricorn and a Taurus get together, they are into stability. You share so many of the same desires, and understand each other so well, that you are perfect mates for each other. Success, hard work, and financial stability is so important to both of you that you're guaranteed to amass a lot of wealth and possessions. Just don't work too hard or take each other for granted.

Two Earth signs are very supportive of each other. Your friendship will be based on mutual effort: You'll set out to do only the things that are most important to both of you. Parent and child Earth signs are homebodies—so don't forget to add some variety and spice to your life.

Capricorn and Gemini:
★ Romance ★ Friends ★ Parent/Child

To be blunt, there is no future for a Capricorn with a Gemini. Capricorns prize order and determination; the basic nature of the Gemini is spontaneous, excitable, scattered. You like to do one thing at a time, take your time and do it well. They like to do five things at once and not finish any of them. Geminis are social, flirty; you are quiet and uncommunicative. Give this up—you'll be much better off alone.

Capricorn and Gemini friends have little in common. You are a workaholic, and they like to hang out with friends. As for parents and children: Geminis need to slow down to make this connection work.

139

Capricorns can tune out the incessant chatter of Geminis and not give them what they need.

Capricorn and Cancer:
★ ★ Romance ★ ★ ★ Friends ★ ★ Parent/Child

A romance between a Capricorn and a Cancer takes a lot of adjustment. Are you willing to put in the effort? You are both financially prudent and love to stay close to home. They are very sensitive and dependent and you are emotionally aloof. On one level, you like their emotional attachment, because it makes you feel safe. But when they start getting overemotional and clingy, you want to dismiss them and get on with things.

Friendships between two opposing signs (see p. 4) are easier to work out than romantic relationships. You know there will always be other friends around to lighten the load. Parents and children of this pairing have different needs and different ways of expressing them. Remember: Extra affection will go a long way with a Cancer.

Capricorn and Leo:
★ Romance ★ Friends ★ ★ Parent/Child

Usually a reserved Capricorn is in no way interested in social and energetic Leo. But if by chance you decided that Leo was worth acquiring, you'd have to do a lot to get one to stick around. Leo is a grand, sweeping romantic you'd have to inundate with gifts and attention. You'd quickly get fed up. After all, you know that the time and money it costs to romance a Leo is a waste. You've got much more important things to do.

You can't imagine ever wanting to be friends with a Leo. They're way too exuberant for your conservative taste. Parents and children have more chance to relate, because they're both loyal signs.

Capricorn and Virgo:
★★★★Romance ★★★★Friends ★★★★Parent/Child

You have met your perfect mate in a Virgo. You're both quiet and reserved, plan your lives carefully, and enjoy spending time alone in your meticulously decorated room. You're both financially conservative, hardworking, and detail-oriented—you corner the market on the hardworking part, Virgo the details. This is going to be a well-paced relationship. Just don't expect it to be exciting.

Two earth signs develop deep and lasting friendships. If you have a Virgo friend, you will always have a safe place to go. Capricorn and Virgo parents and children make great families. They just don't take many risks, together or alone.

Capricorn and Libra:
★ Romance ★ Friends ★ Parent/Child

This is another sign that's not worth getting involved with. You choose your friends and romances carefully, and you're serious about who you spend time with. Libras hang out with everyone. If they could socialize for a living, they would. They're charmers, but you aren't easily mesmerized by glitz and glamour. You'd much prefer a practical mate with feet firmly planted on the ground.

You two don't have enough in common to want to hang out together. If you did, your Libra would surely find something to talk to you about. Capricorn and Libra parents and children will not see eye to eye on much. You work, and they play—it's like apples and oranges.

Capricorn and Scorpio:
★ ★ ★ Romance ★ ★ ★ Friends ★ ★ Parent/Child

If you're up for a good challenge, a Scorpio is for you—as astute as you are cunning, as intense as you are disciplined. This relationship is worth the effort. You like to put everything in a neat little box, but

Scorpios are too powerful and spontaneous, which you will just have to get used to. You'll also have to get used to being more affectionate and emotional.

Friends of this combination share the same ambition and determination. You may have different goals, but respect each other's methods. Capricorn and Scorpio parents and children have different ways of communicating. There's a lot of love there, but you're stubborn, and Scorpios are domineering.

Capricorn and Sagittarius:
★ Romance ★ ★ Friends ★ Parent/Child

Nothing about a Sagittarius gets your goat. Sagittarians love their freedom more than anything. They have a frivolous attitude toward love and a profound need to explore the world. You take your love seriously and don't like to leave home unless it's to accomplish something important. From the beginning you'd see that they never intended to make this a forever thing, and that's when you'd get too overbearing for them to take. Leave them to their wanderings.

Be more optimistic about Capricorn and Sagittarius friendships. Sagittarians don't stay put for too long, but Capricorns are too distracted with important things to notice. Unfortunately, parent/child relations between these two can be chilly. Neither one is very emotional.

Capricorn and Capricorn:
★★Romance★★★Friends★★★Parent/Child

At first you find that another Capricorn makes a very attractive romance, which may even last awhile, but there are tiny things wrong with this that can become way too big over the long haul. The positives: You're both conservative, persistent, and hardworking. The negatives: Capricorns are prone to gloomy moods and find it hard to unwind. Without another sign's influence, this could be deadly.

Two friendly Goats love each other's company. You like people who are exactly like you, but this can get a little boring. Capricorn parents and children will have a stable and secure home. Try to be affectionate and attentive, and remember to play sometimes.

Capricorn and Aquarius:
★Romance★★Friends★Parent/Child

The intelligent and lofty Aquarian might seem perfect for you, but first impressions can be deceiving. Aquarians are too progressive and individualistic for conservative you. They are unpredictable and adventurous, and you're consistent, disciplined. They're also opinionated, as are you—and neither one of you is about to compromise your convictions.

Capricorns and Aquarians make better friends. You are attracted to their dignified demeanor, and they consider everyone a friend. Parents and children of this combination can get mired in their extremely different personalities.

Capricorn and Pisces:
★★★★Romance ★★★★Friends ★★★★Parent/Child

Dreamy Pisces and grounded Capricorn are an ideal pair. Usually you dismiss people who are lazy and delicate, but when you see these qualities in a Pisces, you want to jump in and save them. In return, they will admire your strength and give you lots of love and affection. You may not like their dependency, but you do enjoy being appreciated, so you'll work that out. You're both moody, but Pisces likes to see the best in people, so they'll uplift you.

A friendship between these two is supersupportive. Pisces' creativity can inspire Capricorn's work efforts. Parent/child relationships work well. Capricorns aren't emotional, but Pisces intuitively understands the stuff you're not saying.

AQUARIUS AIR
JANUARY 20–FEBRUARY 18

Aquarius and Aries:
★ ★ ★ Romance ★ ★ ★ ★ Friends ★ ★ ★ Parent/Child

A romance between an Aquarian and an Aries is a dynamic one. Both of you are energetic, independent, and strong-willed. Unfortunately for you, Aries beats you in that last category hands down. You are spontaneous, and Aries is impulsive. You might not like their occasional brashness, but you can be quite cheeky yourself when your opinion is being challenged. If you can handle their need to dominate, you've got yourself a winning relationship. You don't even have to kowtow. Go ahead, give them a good fight—they'll love it!

Friends of this pairing will have a natural bond. Your imagination plus Aries' enthusiasm adds up to one wild time. Parent/child Aquarius/Aries are perfectly matched. You're thinkers, and Aries are doers, but you're a good influence on each other.

Aquarius and Taurus:
★ Romance ★ ★ Friends ★ Parent/Child

This relationship isn't meant to be. You are progressive, quick, unconventional. You love your freedom and your social life. Taureans like the comfort of routine. They're slow-moving, cautious, quiet, and possessive. I'm sure you'll agree that this is a recipe for disaster.

Waterbearer and Bull friends match up better. Taurus is easygoing, and you're friendly. Aquarius and Taurus parents and children are going to run into problems because of their opposing natures. Taureans are overprotective and love appreciation. You're independent and unemotional.

Aquarius and Gemini:
★★★★Romance ★★★★Friends ★★★★Parent/Child

Hook a Gemini and you will never want to go fishing again. You're both quick-minded, fun, and social. Both of you are so up on the latest current events, fads, technology, and celebrities that you'll never lack for good conversation. Always exploring and learning together, you're guaranteed to amass a large amount of knowledge and a large group of fans to share it with.

Friendships between Aquarians and Geminis are just as fun and quick-paced. If every Aquarian had a Gemini friend, they would never be bored. Aquarian and Gemini parents and children have a great understanding of each other and common ways of communicating.

Aquarius and Cancer:
★Romance★ ★Friends★ ★Parent/Child

Other than the fact that you are both human beings, Cancer has no qualities compatible with your own. Aquarians thrive on freedom and independence. Intelligent and airy, you seek a partner who has a progressive, cerebral touch. The only thing you'll get from a Cancer is a heavy dose of affection and dependency. Insecure, they'll demand that you stay close to them at all times. They'd stay close to you, but they hate going out. The only thing this relationship is going to leave you with is an emotional hangover.

It's safe to say that Aquarians and Cancers won't be exploring the universe together, but you like them around, especially if you have a personal problem to solve. Parent/child relations are cool but comfortable. Cancers are understanding and overprotective. You're way too strong to let anyone hamper your unconventional style, but you're easygoing about it most of the time.

Aquarius and Leo:
★ ★Romance★ ★ ★Friends★ ★Parent/Child

Romancing a Leo is fine in the beginning. Your common social nature fans the flames. You'll soon find that they're more trouble than they're worth. They crave attention and will constantly be nudging you for it. They're extravagant, too. You like to spend money, but only on your intellectual and experimental desires. The only thing Leos want to spend it on is themselves. Your very progressive opinion of a Leo: Get over yourself!

Air and fire signs get along very well, so friends of this pairing do much better. For best results: Make sure to share center stage. Parent/child relations can be a success as long as you agree to disagree a lot.

Aquarius and Virgo:
★Romance★ ★Friends★ ★Parent/Child

Dating a Virgo is like sitting on a train bound for nowhere. You're an optimistic explorer, always interested in meeting new people and learning new things. Can you imagine a pessimistic, people-pleasing Virgo constantly following you around, trying to reorganize and perfect your carefree style? Not only that, but if you don't respond, they're sure to get a tad critical. That'll make you feel good, right?!

An Aquarius/Virgo friendship may have more going for it. Someone's got to do those pesky rational things you hate doing. Parents and children of this pairing will have peace as long as Virgos don't try to control your every move.

Aquarius and Libra:
★★★★Romance ★★★★Friends ★★★★Parent/Child

Light Libra and airy Aquarius make a dynamic duo. You live life on the edge, thinking about the world, exploring its dimensions. Libra is all too happy to follow along. You harmonize on so many levels—intellectual, physical, emotional—and you'll have a great time going to the theater and art exhibits.

Friendships between Aquarius and Libra are among the most intellectually stimulating in the universe. Air sign parents are wonderful for air sign children. Nobody understands their smarts and independence more than another air sign.

Aquarius and Scorpio:
★Romance ★★Friends ★★Parent/Child

Dating a Scorpio is like dating your worst nightmare. When you first lay eyes on a Scorpio, you may think their imaginative sense of purpose might make a great companion, but think twice! Scorpios are way too intense and emotional for your airy but obstinate demeanor. Once they're fixated on you, they won't stop until they've overpowered you into submission, and you won't go down without a fight.

Aquarian and Scorpio friendships have better odds. You really do like *everybody*. Parents and children of this match will be unpredictable, but both are compassionate enough to survive.

Aquarius and Sagittarius:
★★★★Romance ★★★★Friends ★★★★Parent/Child

If you want to reinvent romance, go out with a Sagittarian. Both restless and unpredictable, Aquarius and Sagittarius like to explore and philosophize. Living by the rules is out of the question for the Waterbearer and the Archer. Good for you: Sagittarians are so casual about life that they'll let you have your way as long as you're doing something fun and exciting together. Bad for you: They worship freedom and independence more than you do, and they'll never give it up.

Friends of this combination can make even a typing class an adventure. Aquarius and Sagittarius parents and children can overextend yourselves with the fun stuff and not have enough time for the necessities. Sometimes working first and playing later is a positive move.

Aquarius and Capricorn:
★Romance ★ ★Friends ★Parent/Child

If you're a square peg trying to fit into a round hole, then Capricorns are the round peg, fitting in perfectly. Goats are not only reserved and conservative in everything they do, they dislike people who aren't like them. And if you don't know it already, that'd be you. They also like to dominate, not something you particularly like dealing with.

Aquarians and Capricorns might make it as friends if they had common interests, but with progressive Aquarians and workaholic Capricorns, how likely is that? Parent/child pairings would be challenging. You both like to have your way too much to make it easy on one another.

Aquarius and Aquarius:
★★★★Romance★★★★Friends★ ★ ★ Parent/Child

Think about two Aquarians together: smart, inventive, unorthodox, restlessly searching for the key to the universe. If you both have the same ideas of how you should focus all of that lofty thinking, you've got yourself a great match. If you disagree, you'll find yourself in a stalemate: Aquarians are quite fixed in their opinions. The problem is that you are both so busy doing stuff that interests you. When will you have time for each other?

Aquarians are wonderful humanitarians. Two Aquarian friends can save the world together. An Aquarian parent/child relationship may run into a problem: Which of you is more independent and strong-willed? After a couple of hundred challenges you should be able to answer that question.

Aquarius and Pisces:
★★Romance★★★Friends★★Parent/Child

There's better, and there's worse. Aquarians and Pisceans share many similar qualities: You're both creative, idealistic, and visionary. You're lofty humanitarians. Pisces are so compassionate, they'd give away their last dollar to someone in distress. You also have quite different temperaments. You're unemotional, carefree, independent. They're wishy-washy and sensitive, and they can hang on a benevolent Waterbearer like a vine.

These two make perfect friends. You care so much about the world that you can hatch some smart and sassy plans together. Aquarius and Pisces family members can make it as long as Pisces uses intuition to know when enough smothering is enough.

PISCES   WATER
FEBRUARY 19–MARCH 20

Pisces and Aries:
★ Romance ★ ★ Friends ★ Parent/Child

At first glance, the sensitive, receptive Fish and the aggressive, headstrong Ram find each other compelling. But if these two are true to their signs, the powerful Ram will quickly become too overbearing for the emotional Fish. Pisces sees love as the answer to everything, and Aries just likes to be the center of attention.

Aries/Pisces friendships fare pretty well, especially if their Moon and Venus signs are compatible. In friendships, you can enjoy Aries' bursts of energy, then get out before you get run over. Wild Aries is likely to give you a run for your money in parent/child relationships as well.

Pisces and Taurus:
★★★★Romance★★★Friends★★★Parent/Child

Strong, decisive Taurus is just what the Pisces ordered. You tend to be wishy-washy, consulting your friends and loved ones about every detail in your life. Who better to lean on than a passionate, caring, and stable Bull? Creative Pisces appreciates Taurus artistry. Together you can build a perfect hideaway, and both of you would love nothing more than to stay there forever.

Pisces and Taurus friends talk differently. You talk about your problems and feelings, and they discuss money and possessions. Parents and children of this pairing have a very good relationship. You just wish they were better at going with the flow.

Pisces and Gemini:
★ Romance ★ ★ Friends ★ Parent/Child

For sensitive Pisces, dating a Gemini is an emotional catastrophe waiting to happen. You get totally lost in your romances, but cool, independent Geminis move in five directions at once, and they never stay put. You want to live in LaLa Land, but no matter how much you try, they don't want to go there with you. Who will leave the other one first is the question.

Pisces and Gemini friends have more of a chance. You can find enough to talk about to survive. Parent/child Pisces/Geminis don't have an easy time relating. Their chatty nature can seem inconsiderate to you.

Pisces and Cancer:
★★★★Romance ★★★★Friends ★★★★Parent/Child

You can't do better than a Cancer when it comes to an understanding and sympathetic partner. Cancers can be hard to read because their emotions are hidden under the surface, but not for a Pisces. You can tell exactly what they need, and you give it to them. In return you will get a secure and devoted partner who will love doting on you as much as you dote on them. Watch the moods. Between you, you've got more ups and downs than a mood ring has colors.

Pisces and Cancers make the best of friends. No one in the zodiac understands you better. Water sign parents tend to be overprotective, water sign children insecure. Instead of clinging to each other, let in some outside influences.

Pisces and Leo:
★ Romance ★ ★ Friends ★ Parent/Child

A romance with a Leo will be fun until you get to know them. Both of you are creative and passionate. You'll love the Lion's strength and magnetism, but it won't be long before their arrogant and demanding nature pops up. You are introverted, sensitive, and emotional, and you need a partner who understands you for who you are. Leos are too busy being the center of attention.

Pisces and Leo friendships can make it further. The Lion's big energy can give you a boost, and Leos will gladly count you among the members of their court. Pisces and Leo parents and children will constantly run into the same problem: They want to do what they want, and you can't say no, even as you pull out your hair in frustration.

Pisces and Virgo:
★★Romance★★★Friends★★★Parent/Child

Pisces and Virgos are complete opposites. Found on opposite sides of the astrological wheel (see p. 4), these two are really two halves of a whole. This can be a good match for a while, but problems can arise from your need for an emotional connection at all costs, while Virgos tend to be too realistic about the details.

In friendship, the practical Virgo helps to focus Pisces, and intuitive Pisces understands the deeper side of Virgo, the side they never show anyone. Stability is so important to a Virgo that they can get confused by your deep emotional and creative needs. Virgo parents put too much emphasis on organization, but what you really need is a bit of creative chaos.

Pisces and Libra:
★★Romance★★Friends★★Parent/Child

You both have an appreciation of the finer things in life, but this can get you only so far. A few romantic evenings later, you're beginning to open up, to make an emotional attachment, and to demand more time. In return, you'll see them working late, running off to social engagements, and trying their hardest to avoid emotional entrapment. You're way too sensitive for this treatment.

Pisces and Libra can prove better friends than romances. You'll understand each other at one level at least: your affinity for anything artistic and creative. Parents and children of this match will look like a perfect family—at least on the outside. Libras are good at keeping it light, and you're masters of denial.

Pisces and Scorpio:
★★★★Romance★★★★Friends★★★★Parent/Child

These two water signs add up to a most mystical and otherworldly relationship. You have met your intuitive and emotional match in a Scorpio. With them, you can get as mushy and clingy as you want. Scorpios love being the be-all and end-all to their romantic mates, and all their intense energy makes you feel safe and secure. It's good to have someone around to make all the important decisions.

Pisces and Scorpio friends have a deep understanding of each other and empathy for the wrongs of the world. Life with these two water sign parents and children will be intensely psychic, smothering, and compassionate.

Pisces and Sagittarius:
★Romance★ ★Friends★ ★Parent/Child

When a Sagittarius has a romantic eye on you, it's hard to keep your feet on the ground. Their flirting and flattery will entice you right into their arms, but unfortunately, that is as far as your relationship will go. They love to explore and experiment. You're all about emotional commitment, doing everything you can to keep your partners at home, while they do everything they can to stay away. Adding insult to injury: You'd find their straight-shooting tongue hurtful.

Friends with these signs can have a better go of it. Sagittarians are friendly and generous. This you will like, and you'll get your emotional needs met elsewhere. Pisces and Sagittarius parents and children have fundamental problems. You like an environment filled with love and affection, and they like a life of freedom and fun.

Pisces and Capricorn:
★★★★Romance ★★★★Friends ★★★★Parent/Child

Sensitive, dreamy Pisces can find it hard to keep their feet on the ground and their bank account balanced, which just so happen to be Capricorn's greatest strengths. If you're looking for someone to protect you and provide you with nice dates and gifts—two qualities you adore—then search no more. On the other hand, if you want to explore the depths of your sensitivity, Capricorn is likely to fall short in that department.

As a friendship, this relationship works on the same dynamics. The Fish can definitely find more soulful friends, but having a hardworking Goat around reminds you that sometimes accomplishing goals isn't such a bad idea. Parents and children of these signs operate on two different wavelengths, have completely different desires in life, and can have problems communicating this to each other.

To Be or Not to Be

Pisces and Aquarius:
★★Romance★★★Friends★★Parent/Child

You have a lot in common with this air sign, and that can spark your interest, but don't forget that your Aquarian has a basically airy nature—and that's the downfall of this relationship. You love their artistic, eccentric, humanitarian qualities. They love your creativity and sensuality. The problem here is that you want a deep emotional bond, and they like a more intellectual connection. Their need for freedom is too much for you to bear.

Friendships between the Fish and the Waterbearer can be fruitful. They want to advance the world, and you want to heal it. Just don't expect that air of detachment to ever go away. Aquarian parents instill compassion in their children, yet at times may not be able to handle your emotional needs.

Pisces and Pisces:
★★Romance★★★Friends★★★Parent/Child

You and another Pisces would create quite an unforgettable romance, but how long would it last? You are both sensitive, emotional, and dependent. You hate reality and are the zodiac's best at avoiding what you don't want to see. You both love staying at home, spending countless hours in illusionary bliss.

This is fine if one of you happens to be the heir to a fortune. If not, the fantasy can quickly fade.

Two Pisces love hanging out together, and two Pisces in the same family will have a natural ability to communicate. They just need a strong earth sign influence around to get things done.

CHAPTER 5

Beyond the Basics

Here's where you get to delve deeper into who you are, based on astrology. All you need to know is your approximate time of birth, and you can discover which sign the Moon was in at your birth as well as the placement of Mars and Venus in your astrological makeup. Why is this important? Although your Sun sign plays a significant role in who you are, it's not the only aspect that governs your personality, your tastes, emotions, desires, and energy level. Also, you probably have read the Sun sign description of your best friend and felt that it didn't quite describe her with pinpoint accuracy. The underlying influences of

163

the Moon, Venus, and Mars all have a role in making her who she is. By finding out what signs these three heavenly bodies fall into, you will get to know yourself, your friends, and sweethearts to the core.

THE MOON: THE INSIDE YOU

The Moon governs your emotional side, your daily habits, and what's going on in your life under the surface. When you have an important appointment and your car breaks down, what's your initial response? First thing in the morning, do you like to watch the news or listen to music? When you see your loved one flirting with your best friend, what do you think? These are the kinds of things ruled by your Moon sign. Check the chart to find your Moon sign, then read about the lunar influences on your personality. Do the same for those you love.

Reading the Moon Charts

The dates and times listed in the Moon charts on pages 212–274 indicate the times when the Moon changed signs. For example, on January 2, 1969, the Moon moved from Gemini to Cancer at 11:00 A.M. On January 4, 1969, the Moon moved from Cancer into Leo at 11:00 P.M. Eastern time. If you were born on January 3, 1969, you have a Cancer Moon. If you were born on January 4 after 11:00 P.M., you have a Leo Moon.

The times are correct to within 45 minutes. If you're born within one hour of the times listed in these Moon charts, carefully read both signs that border the time change and decide which one fits you best. For example, if your birthday is 9:45 A.M. (Eastern time) on January 7, you must read the descriptions for both Virgo and Leo and pick the one that describes you emotionally. If you do not know your exact time of birth, you can determine your Moon sign this way as well.

The dates and times in all the charts are calculated in the Eastern time zone. You don't need to know whether you were born in standard time or daylight saving time, because those time changes are already figured into the charts. On the other hand, you do need to know what time zone you were born in. If you were born in the Eastern part of the United States, you need to do nothing with these times. If you were born in Central time, subtract one hour from the times listed; for Mountain time, two hours; and for Pacific time, three hours.

Now to look up your Moon sign, go to page 212.

Aries Moon

With energetic Aries influencing the Moon, you're impulsive and independent. You respond to emotional situations as if you're on automatic pilot. Your tolerance level is low. You can blow your top one second, and forget about it the next. You get over it quickly, but other people may not. You also like to do things your own way, whether that is good for you or not. What to do about this: Remember that people are people. What they say isn't always orchestrated to get a rise out of you.

Taurus Moon

Your moods and emotional well-being are directly linked to the security of your money and relationships. A restrained person, you think about all the implications before you respond—but once you've made up your mind, no one can talk you out of it. You're reliable and have good instincts. Don't be surprised if many people lean on you for advice and emotional stability. Keep this in mind: You like to think before you act, but if someone else has a better idea along the way, it's in your best interest to listen.

Beyond the Basics

Gemini Moon

Gemini Moons live in the moment, picking things up and dropping them when something better comes along. You're extroverted and funny, but you use your quick wit to hide the inside you from the world. Emotionally, you switch from one outlook to another and back a million times before lunch. You like to think away your emotions—you're more cerebral than sensitive. Words of wisdom for you: Think twice and carefully. Sit still long enough to figure things out.

Cancer Moon

Moody highs and lows are a way of life for Cancer Moons. You're the most compassionate of people, and are great to be in a relationship with. You love your family and pets, and you enjoy the safety of hanging out close to home. Ladies, watch out: This could mean you've got a closet Mama's boy. Best way to deal with yourself: Keep away from leachy energy-suckers who just want to complain to a good listener.

Leo Moon

Leo Moons find it majorly difficult to contain your thoughts, feelings, and emotions. Large Lions tend to react too quickly and idealistically for your own good. Proud and flamboyant, you can turn a heart-to-heart talk into high drama, and you'll go to any lengths not to appear vulnerable. A suggestion: Keep in touch with your motivations. As long as you keep it real, people will see that your response comes from the best of intentions.

Virgo Moon

Your Moon in Virgo makes you emotionally reserved. You take stock of your situation, analyzing everything before letting your emotions out of the bag, almost as if you're trying to figure out the perfect emotional response before giving any response at all. You can indulge in a bit of self-pity under the surface and tend to be too critical of yourself. The best way to deal with yourself on a deep level: Take a bit more time to accept and appreciate who you are without thinking too much.

Libra Moon

People with the Moon in Libra need beauty and harmony in every aspect of their lives: environment, relationships, and career. What other people, especially your romantic partners, say and do is important to you. You get upset too easily when you're confronted by anger or stress. You'd much rather have everything calm and balanced and will do anything to avoid emotional outbursts. Astrological advice: Trust in a higher power. Maybe then you won't think the weight of the world is on your shoulders every time you have to make a decision.

Scorpio Moon

This is a tough place for the Moon to be. Scorpio Moons are strong-willed and intense, and their feelings are buried deep beneath the surface. Instead of talking about how you feel, you may manipulate others to get what you want. When you don't get it, you can brood for hours trying to find a way to get revenge and get what you deserved in the first place. Otherworldly wisdom: Learn to let go of past hurts. Awaken all of your magnificent powers and use them wisely.

Sagittarius Moon

The Sagittarian straightforward speech mixed with the influences of emotional Moon adds up to someone who can be careless with thoughts and feelings. You love exploring philosophy, but you can be too emotionally attached to beliefs you picked up early in life, which can cloud your thinking. Restless, you are sensitive-phobic, using your sense of humor to deflect deep situations and then leaving before things go too far. Your best astro-philosophy: Exploring the inner you can be as fun as cliff-diving.

Capricorn Moon

Moon in Capricorn makes people ambitious and successful. It doesn't have a deep emotional influence, because Capricorn Moons can be reserved and insecure, and they identify their self-worth with success. Achieving your goals and social status is more important than emotional intimacy. Everything—including relationships—is serious business to you. How to create more emotional balance: Stop worrying about things that may never happen, let go, and enjoy yourself. *Sensitivity* isn't a dirty word.

Aquarius Moon

Aquarians are humanitarians and high-minded philosophers. Having your emotions in this sign makes you idealistic. Because you naturally gravitate toward the bigger picture, it's hard for you to locate your feelings and emotions on a personal level. Your best face is imaginative, intelligent, and offbeat. At your worst you are too rebellious and radical for your own good. The best way to figure yourself out: Don't hold your emotions ransom to your strong need to be individualistic. You can have both the coolness and the warmth.

Pisces Moon

Pisces Moons are extremely sensitive to the thoughts and feelings of others. You may not realize this, but you're unconsciously picking stuff up all over the place. After a few hours with a lot of people, Pisces Moons have the need to withdraw and isolate themselves. You're great at creating a safe fantasyland in which to play, and you look at the rest of the world through those same rose-colored glasses. A fishy recommendation: You can live in LaLa Land *and* be truthful with yourself. Use your intuition, and don't be misled.

VENUS: YOU IN LOVE

The planet Venus indicates how you deal with love in your life. When your sweetheart says "I love you" for the first time, Venus tells you how to respond. When you need to get new clothes and accessories, your Venus sign indicates what you'll buy. Guys can tell what kind of women they like by their Venus sign. The simple chart will reveal your Venus sign. Once you know your love planet, you can read short descriptions of how romantic you are, what kind of clothing you prefer, and what kind of sweethearts you like.

Reading the Venus Charts

The times listed in the charts on pages 203–208 indicate the times when Venus solidly moved from one sign into another. Since Venus is a fast-moving planet, these calculations are as accurate as possible. The four hours before the times listed—the overlapping time it takes for Venus to move into the next sign—is called the cusp. Since Venus is continually moving, we can point to a time when it moves from one piece of the pie to another, but it is not so simple to say when the influence of one sign ends and another begins. The closer you were born to the times listed, the more likely it is that you were born under the new sign.

Here's how to read the Venus charts accurately: If you are born approximately four hours before the times listed, you must read both bordering signs to determine which describes you better at love and play. For example, let's say your best friend was born on February 2, 1969, at 5:00 A.M., and you were born on February 2, 1969, at 8:00 A.M., and you want to figure out your Venus signs. According to the calculations below, your friend's Venus could be either Pisces or Aries, but your Venus is definitely in Aries. Your friend must read both to make an accurate determination. Since Aries was in full swing at 7:52 A.M. (Eastern time), your Venus sign is distinctly Aries.

The dates and times in all the charts are based on the Eastern time zone. You don't need to know whether you were born in standard time or daylight saving time, because those time changes are already figured into the charts. On the other hand, you do need to know what time zone you were born in. If you were born in the Eastern part of the United States, you need to do nothing with these times. If you were born in Central time, subtract one hour from the times listed; for Mountain time, delete two hours, and Pacific Time, three hours.

Now go to page 203 to find your Venus sign!

Venus in Aries

Venus in Aries indicates that you're outgoing and impulsive with friends and romances. You go after what you want no matter what anyone else thinks—and this can be a problem if that anyone is the one you want. You fall in love at first sight and are very passionate. Just watch your tendency to be impulsive and you won't get yourself in trouble.

Venus-Aries people are power dressers. You like

to be the center of attention and want your clothing to express your wild energy. Guys with Venus in Aries like women—all kinds of women. When you see one you like, you like to spend a grand amount of time and energy getting her. (Hint: Girls, that means you should play hard to get!)

Venus in Taurus

Sensitive and affectionate, people with Venus in Taurus hope their love will be lasting and secure. You're cautious and take things slowly, but once you fall in love, you fall with all your heart. You like to possess your mates and have quite a jealous streak when you feel your relationship's security is on the line.

You like beautiful things, but appreciate value and money. Down-to-earth, you like to dress well and functionally at the same time. Old Navy is definitely the store for you. If you're a guy, you want a woman who is adoring and available, someone who will loyally stick by you and love you forever.

Beyond the Basics

Venus in Gemini

Boy, do people with Venus in Gemini have a good time! You love to socialize, go to parties, and hop from one romance to another. All your curiosity and interests make it hard for you to settle down. When you do, love will just be one part of your busy life. Venus-Gemini people keep love on the light side. You hate getting caught up in deep emotional issues.

People with Venus in Gemini have an eye for the hottest trends, so you have a closet full of hip, cutting-edge clothes; everyone else takes their fashion cues from you. Guys with Venus in Gemini like fun, witty, creative women who have independence, style, and class.

Venus in Cancer

Venus in Cancer means that you're deeply sensitive and romantic, but you hide that fact well under your tough defensive shell. All of your love and affection doesn't color your need for a safe home and financial security. Tentative by nature, you need a devoted sweetie to give you tons of reassurances that you're their one and only. Once you feel good about it, you cozy up to your romance and never want to let it go.

You really couldn't care less about your clothing. Yes, you want to look nice, but it's your home that you want to furnish comfortably. Guys with the planet Venus in Cancer are looking for a stay-at-home girlfriend: a sensitive, sweet girl they can take home to mother.

Venus in Leo

Outgoing, extravagant, and romantic, people with Venus in Leo do everything with a theatrical flair. You definitely like to get noticed by members of the opposite sex. Venus-Leos love being the center of attention (you like to show off your mate, too). You can flirt, but your romantic interest can't. If they do, they'll have to deal with your jealous streak.

Your appearance must be dramatic as well, and above all you value luxury. When you see something and you decide you can't live without it, you find a way to get it, no matter how much it costs. A guy with Venus in the sign of Leo likes passionate, social women with striking hair who dress well from head to toe.

Venus in Virgo

Having Venus in Virgo makes you cautious and analytical in love. You think first, love later. When your perfectionist attitude is focused on your romances, you can easily find fault with everything. It's not that you *want* to—you're so detail-oriented, you just can't help it. Also, you don't like to fall in love too quickly, just in case you see that your mate isn't living up to your high standards.

You are always impeccably dressed, down to the last detail. Your clothes reflect your understated grace and your knowledge of fashion. Venus-Virgo guys need a woman who is smart, reserved, well-dressed, and loyal.

Venus in Libra

If you have Venus in Libra, lucky you! Venus is the ruling planet of Libra, and that makes it right at home. You're a most gracious and refined mate. You do everything right—from setting up the perfect date, to bringing the perfect token of affection, to giving the perfect kiss. Your clothing and accessories are beautiful. Everything is worn with a touch of class—every hair in place, every detail taken into account, down to your shoelaces.

Venus-Libra guys may be looking for something hard to find, a mate with the same degree of elegance. What to do about that? Take over the details, teach your mate your secrets, and your relationship is sure to be pleasing.

Venus in Scorpio

If you have Venus in Scorpio, you are intense, creative, secretive, and dominant. You fall in love headfirst and deeply, letting your emotions carry you away. You want your mates to go there with you, and if they don't, you can have a problem seeing their point of view. Watch out when your stubborn possessiveness comes out of the closet.

You like spending time and money only to do things that are important to you. You think extravagant clothing is superficial. You'd rather your gear reflect the inner you. You may even dress like a slob and have tons of money in your pockets for higher pursuits. Men with Venus in Scorpio are attracted to girls who are intuitive and extreme.

Venus in Sagittarius

Love from people with Venus in Sagittarius expresses itself in polish and sophistication. You are well read, well educated, and have a wide-reaching influence. Social climbing is a sport to Venus-Sag people—you can share your love of the finer things with everyone you meet. Best way to approach this side of you: When you first meet someone, ask yourself, "Is there love with this magnetism, or is it the magnetism that I love?"

You dress to kill. You're extravagant, cheery, and well put together. Whatever you wear, it will be original and unforgettable. Guys with Venus in Sag: You like a woman who is adventurous but has the same philosophy and religious beliefs as you do.

Venus in Capricorn

Venus in Capricorn gives you a cool demeanor. In love, you're loyal and dependable, but you like to achieve a certain amount of success and security before you allow yourself to surrender to pleasure. You like to fall in love with people who have money or high social standing. This makes it easier to let go and have a good time knowing you're well taken care of.

Your clothing reflects your private and dignified manner, showing the world your fine taste and strong sense of personal style. Guys with Venus in Capricorn like graceful, reserved women who have an interest in their career and are completely devoted to them.

Venus in Aquarius

People with Venus in Aquarius attract love from many places. You're friendly and popular, light-hearted and aloof. You take an unconventional and cerebral approach to love, and like to avoid emotional and passionate outbursts, preferring to think about things rather than feel them. Don't be possessive or jealous of a Venus in Aquarius. It makes the natives restless.

You like what you wear to reflect your offbeat nature. You don't care if something is expensive or secondhand, as long as it's cool. Venus-Aquarius guys like a woman they can have a great friendship with—someone who is independent, social, and unique.

Venus in Pisces

A sensitive Piscean influence on Venus makes you an intuitive and emotional mate. You love to be in love and will do anything to keep it—including giving too much of yourself or refusing to see the negatives of your relationship. You have so much compassion that it borders on self-sacrifice, putting others' happiness before your own.

You have an artistic and sensual style, preferring clothing that is soft to the touch and to the eye. From the color to the fabric, your clothing says "Love me." For guys, having Venus in Pisces means that you are attracted to sensitive and loving partners who will make you feel safe and warm inside and out.

MARS: YOU AT PLAY

Mars expresses your wild side—what you have passion for, how you approach projects and interests, and for girls, what you look for in a sweetheart. What are your favorite sports? What kinds of careers are perfect for you? What topics spur you into action? The sign your Mars is placed in makes a big difference in the answers to these questions.

One look at the Mars chart and you'll know what sign the planet Mars falls into in your horoscope. Read the explanation of your approach to school, work, hobbies, and friends!

Reading the Mars Charts

The times listed in the charts on pages 209–211 indicate the times when Mars solidly moved from one sign into another. These times are accurate to within about an hour. The one hour before the times listed is the cusp. If you were born one hour before the times listed, to read these Mars charts accurately, you must read both bordering signs to determine which describes you better at play.

The times in all the charts are based on the Eastern time zone. You don't need to know whether you were born in standard time or daylight saving time, because those time changes are already figured into the charts. On the other hand, you do need to know what time zone you were born in. If you were born in the Eastern part of the United States, you need to do nothing with these times. If you were born in Central time, subtract one hour from the times listed below; for Mountain time, two hours; and Pacific time, three hours.

Now go to page 209 to determine your Mars sign!

Mars in Aries

Action planet Mars is the ruler of Aries, the most assertive of the signs. This makes you a goal-driven, action-oriented person, but it can also make you aggressive. If you find yourself hotheaded sometimes, this is the reason! You approach everything with a zest and an energy level unseen in any of the other signs, and you love to play. Problems come up when you want to play and others don't. That's when you can bulldoze unsuspecting mellow people. The more competitive and energetic your hobbies are, the better—karate, taebo, or a wild pickup game on the basketball courts. How to handle yourself best: When you interact with others, take a deep breath before you speak.

Girls with Mars in Aries: You appreciate strong guys who can give you a run for your money. This can make every day an adventure, but you can expect a lot of head-butting!

Mars in Taurus

Having Mars force focused on Taurus desire for money and possessions makes you extremely determined to succeed in life. You're slow to move, but once you figure out what you want to do, you won't stop until you succeed—big time! Mars also magnifies Taurus' stubborn nature. If you don't get what you want you can be downright bullish.

You're great at constructing ornate objects and furniture with an earthy overtone. You can sit for hours working on the tiniest detail. Your concentration is amazing. In sports, you may not be the fastest person on the team, but you've got the most perseverance. Women with Mars in Taurus like a guy who is passionate and devoted and who will drive for the top.

Mars in Gemini

With Mars in Gemini, it's all in your head. You have a sharp and active mind, a mental aggressiveness. You're quick at understanding new things and have an uncanny power with words. Mars also doubles the standard Gemini restlessness. Thinking is one thing, and doing is another. Making a final decision and taking decisive action is hard for Mars-Gemini folks.

You excel at activities that summon up cerebral courage: debating, politics, physics, and journalism. Don't take on projects that take tons of focus and follow-through—you lose interest too quickly. Female Mars-Geminis like their counterparts to be intelligent, quick-witted, and persuasive—someone they can talk to all night and never get bored with.

Mars in Cancer

People with Mars in Cancer are prone to intense mood swings. Mars agitates the already sensitive emotions of Cancer and causes eruptions deep under the surface. Cancer governs the home, so Mars-Cancer moods can easily affect your relationship with your parents and romances. Words of wisdom: If you're unhappy in a relationship, do some thinking and talking along with your brooding.

Mars-Cancer people are handy around the house. Fixing and reorganizing things is your forte. You're an emotionally energized artist and creator as well. Just don't join the military—there's no room there for your moody outbursts. Women with Mars in Cancer like guys who are emotionally supercharged. Lots of fights, but lots of making up. Mmmmm!

Beyond the Basics

Mars in Leo

Mars in Leo makes for one hot-blooded individual! Passionate, willful, and dynamic, everything you do is infused with power, authority, and flair. Mars-Leo people are natural leaders and entertainers, always on the front lines of the event. Just a little warning: Watch the ego. Here it can be big *and* active.

Your activities and hobbies are competitive and energetic. You like team sports better than individual ones, and you'll manage to be the captain of the team every time. You also love to woo members of the opposite sex. Women Mars-Leos like a guy who is powerful and passionate—the ultimate male specimen— except that you like to dominate as well. This should be fun to observe.

Mars in Virgo

If you have Mars in Virgo, you are detail-oriented and precise. Your work habits are calculated, methodical, and exact. You'll work only in the most organized of environments. You're great at doing arduous research and calculations. If anyone can account for every last decimal point, it's you. You can't stand sloppy work habits in other people and don't hesitate to tell them so.

Hobbies of this exacting nature suit you to a T.

Computer games, investing in stocks, and chess are a few things you excel in. Women with Mars in Virgo like fellow perfectionists, basically methodical workaholics whose passions are kept under wraps.

Mars in Libra

If you have Mars in Libra, you love to throw parties, plan dates, and coordinate social events. You're the perfect host and conversationalist, and you thrive on all the appreciation you get for your social efforts. On a more aggressive note, Mars-Libra people have a compelling need for fairness, and you can get angry when you hear of unfair situations, whether they're yours or someone else's.

You add a refined elegance to all activities you undertake, whether you're working out or walking through the mall. You're good at physical activities that require intelligence and social skills: golf, tennis, tai chi, or lunch. Women with this placement are attracted to beaus who are sophisticated, artistic, and popular.

Mars in Scorpio

People with Mars in Scorpio have deep emotions, strong commitments, and intense desires. Whatever you want, you go after it with disciplined force, calculating every step and wasting no time or energy in the process. Because of the all-or-nothing vibe, Mars-Scorpio people make either loyal friends or bad enemies, depending upon which side you end up on. On a bad day you can be secretive, jealous, and obstinate.

Fascinated by intrigue, action, and danger, you are into competitive sports in which you get to play mind games: laser tag, ice hockey, and heli-skiing. Women with Mars in Scorpio like emotional, creative, intellectually forceful guys who take risks for a living.

Mars in Sagittarius

Mars in Sagittarius will give you courage and independence. You have strong beliefs and you fight for what you believe in—sometimes too much. People can get annoyed at you for trying to convert them to your way of thinking. Bubbling over with enthusiasm, you shoot for your goals like only the Archer can, but you do things in short spurts. To you, all commitments are toxic.

You love outdoor sports. You play hard, and you play by the rules. Going to the park on the weekend for a game of touch football, soccer, or basketball is your favorite. Nothing too organized, though—you'd much prefer to come and go as you please. Women with Mars in Sagittarius like their counterparts to be fun-loving, independent, and emotionally detached.

Mars in Capricorn

Energetic Mars gives Capricorn's methodical nature a kick in the pants and magnifies Capricorn's workaholic, playaholic nature. You use your energy wisely, but only on tasks you wish to accomplish, not on hobbies—that is, unless they will help further your goals. Your energy is less raw physical energy than it is mental, and because of that, you have great ability to achieve concrete results.

Your best interests are those in which you can have fun and win, too. Running on the track team, joining a chess club, and buying stocks are all things that get your goat! Women with Mars in Capricorn like a cunning and energetic guy by their side, someone with the same potential as they have. Beware of all work and no play in your relationship.

Mars in Aquarius

Mars in Aquarius drives you to pursue unusual goals. You're always involved with tons of group projects—especially those that improve the world. You have such a quick mind and nonconformist attitude that you go through life rejecting existent systems whether you have better ideas or not! You're a unique blend of social and introspective, and your mind plays a game of tug-of-war between the two.

You're just as likely to begin a crusade to clean up your neighborhood as you are to go for a run. Either way, your mind is always at work developing innovations for the world. Mars-Aquarius women like their guys to be really smart, question authority, and have a humanitarian bent.

Mars in Pisces

People with Mars in Pisces have a deep intuition and active imagination. In fact, you're a big psychic receptor, picking up thoughts and feelings from every person, place, and thing you come in contact with. You're great at using these in your artistic endeavors, but you can get overloaded by them as well. Mars-Pisces people need plenty of rest to keep their emotional balance.

Harsh physical activity isn't your favorite thing. You're attracted to anything artistic—painting, drawing, acting, writing; and anything otherworldly—psychic phenomena, palm reading, past lives, aliens, and ghosts. Girls with Mars in Pisces like their guys to be supersensitive, emotional, creative people who appreciate the arts.

MEN ARE FROM MARS,
WOMEN ARE FROM VENUS

By now this is a cliché, but it's really true. When you use astrology to discover a relationship's compatibility, comparing the couple's Mars and Venus signs will tell you a lot about their romantic nature.

There are two ways to do this. The first is to compare the guy's Mars sign to the girl's Venus sign. This is what you'll be doing for the Romance Compatibility Chart on the following pages. Here's how to do it: If you're a girl, find your Venus sign on the Venus chart, then find your beau's Mars sign on the Mars chart. If you're a guy, look up your Mars sign first, then your sweetie's Venus sign. Then go back to chapter 4: "To Be or Not to Be." Look under the section for your Venus or Mars sign and read about the two signs and their compatibility. See how many stars that pairing received.

The second way to compare Mars and Venus is to separately review the guy's Venus and the girl's Mars. You can tell a lot about the kinds of people you and your mate are attracted to by what signs Mars and Venus fall under. A woman's Mars tells her what type of guy she likes, and a guy's Venus indicates what he likes in a girl.

If you're a girl, read your Mars sign and ask yourself, "Does this accurately describe my sweetheart?" and "Can this guy be what I need in a mate?" Then look up your guy's Venus sign and ask yourself, "Does this sound like me?"; "Can I be this person for him?" If you're a guy, look up your Venus sign and your sweetie's Mars sign and ask yourself the same things. Your answers to these questions tell you a lot about how this relationship will go.

Another aspect of a great romance is being friends with your sweetheart. To compare the friendship side of your relationship—your energy level, the activities that spur you into action, and your hobbies—compare your Mars signs with each other. Look at your Venus signs to see similarities in your tastes for clothing. The more ways you look at your romance through astrology, the more accurate picture you'll receive.

CHAPTER 6

Putting It All Together

Now that you've got the different characteristics of the Sun, Moon, Venus, and Mars straight, use your knowledge of these bodies and signs to compose an accurate profile of yourself and those around you. You can also find out the overall compatibility of a friend or romantic interest.

As you read through each chapter, you probably found that not all of your signs and their individual characteristics were in sync. Maybe your Sun sign makes you outgoing, but your Moon sign makes you crave peace and quiet. This is the way astrology works. It may be confusing at first, but these subtle differences make us interesting and unique. You may be shy at love but fierce at play. On a bad day, these aspects act as conflicting forces. On a good day, one plays down the effects of the other. Conflicting aspects make us fascinating! When you compile all the info and look at it as a whole, you'll understand which aspects take over during what experiences.

Here are three charts that you can use to compile the different aspects. This way, you can easily read about your personality and discover your relationship and friendship compatibility, using the information about all four bodies.

PERSONALITY CHART

This is easy. First, check out your Sun sign description in chapter 2, "You Are Who You Are." Reread it and finish the sentences in the first part of the chart. Then look up your Moon, Venus, and Mars signs in chapter 5, "Beyond the Basics." Reread them, and then finish the sentences. Your personality is the sum of all of these different aspects.

✿ₒ✿ PERSONALITY CHART ✿ₒ✿

Your Name:
Birthday:
My Sun sign is:
My element is:
My personality is:
On a bad day I can be:
What is important to me is:

My Moon sign is:
Emotionally, I am:
Privately, inside I am:

My Venus sign is:
In love I am:
I like to dress like:
Male: I am attracted to these romantic qualities
in the opposite sex:

My Mars sign is:
At play I am:
My energy and interests are:
Female: I am attracted to these romantic qualities
    in the opposite sex:

COMPATIBILITY CHARTS

Sometimes we get too wrapped up in identifying compatibility only by our Sun signs—and that's not the total picture. Earlier in the book, when you read about your first love, you may have been surprised that your Sun signs were awful matches. On a second look, you found that your Mars and Venus were perfect together. That is why you got along so well. It's the overall score that counts the most for compatibility.

Here are two compatibility charts, one for romance and one for friendships. The information you need for the relationship chart is: both sets of Sun, Moon, and Venus signs; the compatibility between the two; and your Mars/Venus connection. For friendships, you need both sets of Sun, Moon, Venus, and Mars signs and a comparison of their compatibility with yours. You can quickly find the compatibility between Moon, Mars, and Venus by looking them up in chapter 4: "To Be or Not to Be."

IT'S IN THE STARS: ADDING UP YOUR OVERALL COMPATIBILITY

Before you start looking up all the specific aspects to fill out your compatibility chart, there is a great way to discover your overall compatibility using the ratings system in the compatibility section.

Since overall compatibility is what you're looking for, you can add up the number of stars in the different compatibility categories on your chart and find out the overall quality of the relationship. After you've completed your compatibility chart, add up the number of stars in the bottom section and see what group it falls under.

14–16 Stars—A match made in heaven. This is so perfect that very few relationships fall into this category. If yours is one of them, congratulations! This is a supportive union. Your thoughts and motivations are in perfect harmony, and you often want the same things out of life. Your ability to understand each other is awesome.

10–13 Stars—Very good compatibility. Most good relationships will fall into this category. Relationships that fall into this grouping are built on mutual love and respect. It just takes a little bit of effort to understand your differences. It is those differences that make the relationship fun. The key to success: Appreciate each other's strengths and forgive each other's weaknesses!

7–9 Stars—This relationship is fine in the short run, but may take more energy than it's worth. If this is a romantic relationship, you'll find that once you get past the surface, you may not have a lot in common. A friendship is fine between these two—it just won't be very deep. Parent/child relationships with this number: You've got your work cut out for you. The good thing is, you have love on your side.

4–6 Stars—Three words: Give it up! Actually, this is not a likely combination, because usually people who are in relationships and friendships are there for a reason, and there's very little in common between these two. If this is a parent/child relationship, it's like Mac versus IBM—you'll have to work at the translation.

HOW DO YOU MATCH UP?

Make a chart for these celebrities, and see what kind of relationship you have together:

BRANDY	February 11, 1979
JENNIFER LOVE HEWITT	February 21, 1979
SARAH MICHELLE GELLAR	April 14, 1977
LUKAS HAAS	April 16, 1976
PRINCE WILLIAM	June 21, 1982
BEN AFFLECK	August 15, 1972, 2:53 A.M. Pacific time
ALICIA SILVERSTONE	October 4, 1976
MATT DAMON	October 8, 1970
LEONARDO DiCAPRIO	November 11, 1974, 2:47 A.M. Pacific time
ISAAC HANSON	November 17, 1980
TIGER WOODS	December 30, 1975, 10:50 P.M. Pacific time

✿ ˳ ✿ ROMANCE COMPATIBILITY ✿ ˳ ✿ CHART

Your Name:	Your Mate's Name:
Birthday:	Birthday:
Sun sign and element:	Sun sign and element:
My personality is:	His/Her personality is:
Number of Sun sign compatibility stars:	Together, we do this for each other:
Moon sign:	Moon sign:
Emotionally, I am:	Emotionally, he/she is:
Number of Moon sign compatibility stars:	Emotionally, we do this for each other:
Venus sign:	Venus sign:
In love I am:	In love he/she is:
Number of Venus sign compatibility stars:	In love, we do this for each other:

Venus/Mars compatibility stars
(Girl's Venus to Guy's Mars):

I like mates that are: He/She likes mates that
are:

Together we do this for each other:

Is it in the stars?
Number of Sun sign compatibility stars:
Number of Moon sign compatibility stars:
Number of Venus sign compatibility stars:
Romance Mars/Venus compatibility stars:

Total Number of Stars:
Overall Compatibility:

⁂⁂⁂ FRIENDSHIP COMPATIBILITY ⁂⁂⁂
CHART

Your Name: Your Friend's Name:

Birthday: Birthday:

Sun sign and   Sun sign and
element: element:

My personality is: His/Her personality is:

Number of Sun sign   Together, we do this
compatibility stars: for each other:

Moon sign: Moon sign:

Emotionally, I am: Emotionally, he/she is:

Number of Moon   Emotionally, we do this
sign compatibility   for each other:
stars:

Venus sign: Venus sign:

In love I am:

In love he/she is:

Number of Venus sign compatibility stars:

Together, we nurture each other this way:

Mars sign:

Mars sign:

I spend my energy doing:

He/She spends her energy doing:

At play I am:

At play he/she is:

Number of Mars sign compatibility stars:

Physically, we do this for each other:

Is it in the stars?
    Number of Sun sign compatibility stars:
    Number of Moon sign compatibility stars:
    Number of Venus sign compatibility stars:
    Number of Mars sign compatibility stars:

        Total Number of Stars:
        Overall Compatibility:

1969

Jan 1	12:00A	Aquarius
Jan 5	1:57A	Pisces
Feb 2	7:52A	Aries
Jun 6	2:30P	Taurus
Jul 7	2:59P	Gemini
Aug 3	7:49P	Leo
Sep 22	10:10P	Virgo
Oct 17	9:45P	Libra
Nov 10	10:19P	Scorpio
Dec 4	11:54P	Sagittarius
Dec 29	1:29A	Capricorn

1971

Jan 8	2:07A	Sagittarius
Feb 6	4:01A	Capricorn
Mar 5	5:48A	Aquarius
Mar 30	7:26A	Pisces
Apr 24	9:05A	Aries
May 19	11:44A	Taurus
Jun 13	1:22P	Gemini
Jul 7	2:57P	Cancer
Aug 1	4:35P	Leo
Aug 25	6:10P	Virgo
Sep 18	7:45P	Libra
Oct 11	9:19P	Scorpio
Nov 5	9:58P	Sagittarius
Nov 29	11:32P	Capricorn
Dec 24	1:07A	Aquarius

1970

Jan 22	3:03A	Aquarius
Feb 15	4:38A	Pisces
Mar 11	6:16A	Aries
Apr 4	7:47A	Taurus
Apr 28	10:22A	Gemini
May 23	12:00P	Cancer
Jun 17	1:39P	Leo
Jul 13	3:21P	Virgo
Aug 9	5:08P	Libra
Sep 8	7:10P	Scorpio

1972

Jan 17	2:42A	Pisces
Feb 11	4:20A	Aries
Mar 8	6:07A	Taurus
Apr 4	7:49A	Gemini
May 11	11:15A	Cancer
Jun 12	1:21P	Gemini
Aug 7	5:02P	Cancer
Sep 8	7:08P	Leo
Oct 5	8:59P	Virgo
Oct 30	9:37P	Libra
Nov 24	11:16P	Scorpio
Dec 19	12:50A	Sagittarius

VENUS CHARTS
(EST & EDT)
♀

1973

Jan 12	2:25A	Capricorn
Feb 5	4:00A	Aquarius
Mar 1	5:34A	Pisces
Mar 25	7:09A	Aries
Apr 19	8:47A	Taurus
May 13	11:22A	Gemini
Jun 6	12:53P	Cancer
Jul 1	2:35P	Leo
Jul 25	4:14A	Virgo
Aug 20	5:52P	Libra
Sep 14	7:31P	Scorpio
Oct 9	9:13P	Sagittarius
Nov 5	10:00P	Capricorn
Dec 8	12:06A	Aquarius

1975

Jan 7	2:03P	Aquarius
Jan 31	3:38P	Pisces
Feb 24	5:13A	Aries
Mar 20	6:47A	Taurus
Apr 14	8:26A	Gemini
May 10	11:08A	Cancer
Jun 7	12:59P	Leo
Jul 10	3:09P	Virgo
Sep 3	6:46P	Leo
Oct 4	8:52P	Virgo
Nov 9	10:14P	Libra
Dec 8	12:04A	Scorpio

1974

Jan 30	3:35A	Capricorn
Mar 1	5:33A	Aquarius
Apr 7	7:59A	Pisces
May 5	10:49A	Aries
Jun 1	12:36P	Taurus
Jul 22	3:57P	Gemini
Aug 15	5:32P	Leo
Sep 9	7:10P	Virgo
Oct 2	8:45P	Libra
Oct 27	2:19P	Scorpio
Nov 19	10:54P	Sagittarius
Dec 14	12:29A	Capricorn

1976

Jan 2	1:43A	Sagittarius
Jan 27	3:21A	Capricorn
Feb 20	4:56A	Aquarius
Mar 15	8:34A	Pisces
Apr 9	8:09A	Aries
May 3	10:44A	Taurus
May 28	12:22P	Gemini
Jun 21	1:57P	Cancer
Jul 15	3:31P	Leo
Aug 9	5:10P	Virgo
Sep 2	6:45P	Libra
Sep 26	9:00P	Scorpio
Oct 20	9:58P	Sagittarius
Nov 14	10:36P	Capricorn
Dec 10	10:15A	Aquarius

VENUS CHARTS
(EST & EDT)
♀

1977

Jan 5	1:57A	Pisces
Feb 3	3:52A	Aries
Jun 7	1:01P	Taurus
Jul 7	2:59P	Gemini
Aug 3	4:45P	Cancer
Aug 29	6:28P	Leo
Sep 22	8:10P	Virgo
Oct 16	10:41P	Libra
Nov 9	1:16A	Scorpio
Dec 3	11:54P	Sagittarius
Dec 28	1:25A	Capricorn

1979

Jan 8	2:07P	Sagittarius
Feb 6	4:02A	Capricorn
Mar 4	5:44A	Aquarius
Mar 30	7:20A	Pisces
Apr 18	8:42A	Aries
May 18	11:44A	Taurus
Jun 12	1:18P	Gemini
Jul 7	2:57P	Cancer
Jul 31	4:36P	Leo
Aug 24	6:10P	Virgo
Sep 18	7:45P	Libra
Oct 11	9:19P	Scorpio
Nov 4	9:54P	Sagittarius
Nov 28	11:29P	Capricorn
Dec 23	1:03A	Aquarius

1978

Jan 21	3:01A	Aquarius
Feb 14	4:32A	Pisces
Mar 10	6:09A	Aries
Apr 3	7:40A	Taurus
Apr 28	9:22A	Gemini
May 22	12:04P	Cancer
Jun 17	1:39P	Leo
Jul 12	3:22P	Virgo
Aug 9	5:08P	Libra
Sep 8	7:06P	Scorpio

1980

Jan 16	4:42A	Pisces
Feb 10	4:16A	Aries
Mar 7	5:59A	Taurus
Apr 4	7:49A	Gemini
May 13	11:23A	Cancer
Jun 6	12:58P	Gemini
Aug 7	5:02P	Cancer
Sep 8	8:08A	Leo
Oct 4	8:55P	Virgo
Oct 30	9:37P	Libra
Nov 24	12:16A	Scorpio
Dec 19	12:50A	Sagittarius

1981

Jan 11	5:25A	Capricorn
Feb 4	8:00A	Aquarius
Feb 28	8:34A	Pisces
Mar 25	7:09A	Aries
Apr 18	8:44A	Taurus
May 12	11:18A	Gemini
Jun 6	12:57P	Cancer
Jun 30	2:35P	Leo
Jul 25	4:10P	Virgo
Aug 19	5:49P	Libra
Sep 13	7:27P	Scorpio
Oct 8	9:14P	Sagittarius
Nov 5	10:02P	Capricorn
Dec 9	12:10A	Aquarius

1983

Jan 6	2:00A	Aquarius
Jan 30	3:34A	Pisces
Feb 23	5:09A	Aries
Mar 20	6:47A	Taurus
Apr 14	8:26A	Gemini
May 10	11:08A	Cancer
Jun 7	12:59P	Leo
Jul 11	3:13P	Virgo
Aug 28	6:22P	Leo
Oct 5	9:56P	Virgo
Nov 9	10:14P	Libra
Dec 7	12:00A	Scorpio

1982

Jan 24	3:11A	Capricorn
Mar 3	5:41A	Aquarius
Apr 7	7:59P	Pisces
May 5	10:50A	Aries
May 31	12:32P	Taurus
Jun 26	2:15P	Gemini
Jul 21	3:53P	Cancer
Aug 15	5:32P	Leo
Sep 8	7:06P	Virgo
Oct 1	10:45P	Libra
Oct 26	12:20A	Scorpio
Nov 18	10:50P	Sagittarius
Dec 13	12:25P	Capricorn

1984

Jan 1	4:42A	Sagittarius
Jan 26	3:17A	Capricorn
Feb 19	9:56A	Aquarius
Mar 15	6:31A	Pisces
Apr 8	8:05A	Aries
May 2	3:44A	Taurus
May 27	12:18P	Gemini
Jun 20	2:57P	Cancer
Jul 15	3:32P	Leo
Aug 8	5:06P	Virgo
Sep 1	10:45P	Libra
Sep 25	8:19A	Scorpio
Oct 20	12:58A	Sagittarius
Nov 13	10:33P	Capricorn
Dec 9	1:15A	Aquarius

VENUS CHARTS
(EST & EDT)
♀

1985

Jan 4	4:58A	Pisces
Feb 3	3:52A	Aries
Jun 7	12:01P	Taurus
Jul 7	2:59P	Gemini
Aug 3	4:46P	Cancer
Aug 28	9:00P	Leo·
Sep 21	11:07P	Virgo
Oct 16	9:41P	Libra
Nov 9	10:16P	Scorpio
Dec 3	11:51P	Sagittarius
Dec 28	1:25A	Capricorn

1987

Jan 8	2:08A	Sagittarius
Feb 6	4:02A	Capricorn
Mar 4	5:44A	Aquarius
Mar 29	7:32A	Pisces
Apr 23	10:02A	Aries
May 18	11:40A	Taurus
Jun 12	1:19P	Gemini
Jul 6	2:53P	Cancer
Jul 31	4:32P	Leo
Aug 24	6:06P	Virgo
Sep 17	7:41P	Libra
Oct 10	9:16P	Scorpio
Nov 3	9:50P	Sagittarius
Dec 23	1:04A	Aquarius

1986

Jan 21	3:00A	Aquarius
Feb 14	4:34A	Pisces
Mar 10	6:09A	Aries
Apr 3	7:44P	Taurus
Apr 27	10:18A	Gemini
May 22	11:57A	Cancer
Jun 16	1:35P	Leo
Jul 12	3:18P	Virgo
Aug 8	5:04P	Libra
Sep 8	7:07P	Scorpio

1988

Jan 16	2:38A	Pisces
Feb 10	4:17A	Aries
Mar 7	5:59A	Taurus
Apr 4	8:50A	Gemini
May 18	11:43A	Cancer
May 28	12:23P	Gemini
Aug 7	8:02A	Cancer
Sep 8	7:09P	Leo
Oct 4	8:55P	Virgo
Oct 29	10:34P	Libra
Nov 23	11:12P	Scorpio
Dec 18	12:47A	Sagittarius

1989

Jan 11	2:21A	Capricorn
Feb 4	3:56A	Aquarius
Feb 28	5:31A	Pisces
Mar 24	7:05A	Aries
Apr 17	9:40A	Taurus
May 11	3:18A	Gemini
Jun 5	12:53P	Cancer
Jun 30	2:32P	Leo
Jul 24	6:10P	Virgo
Aug 18	7:49P	Libra
Sep 13	7:27P	Scorpio
Oct 8	9:10P	Sagittarius
Nov 5	10:00P	Capricorn
Dec 11	12:18A	Aquarius

1969

Jan 1	12:00A	Scorpio
Feb 26	5:22A	Sagittarius
Sep 21	8:02P	Capricorn
Nov 4	9:56P	Aquarius
Dec 16	12:37A	Pisces

1970

Jan 25	3:15A	Aries
Mar 8	6:01A	Taurus
Apr 19	8:46A	Gemini
Jun 4	12:48P	Cancer
Jul 19	3:45P	Leo
Sep 4	6:54P	Virgo
Oct 20	9:56P	Libra
Dec 7	12:01A	Scorpio

1971

Jan 24	3:10A	Scorpio
Mar 13	6:19A	Capricorn
May 4	10:44A	Aquarius
Nov 6	10:02P	Pisces
Dec 27	1:19A	Aries

1972

Feb 11	4:20A	Taurus
Mar 28	7:22A	Gemini
May 13	11:23A	Cancer
Jun 29	2:28P	Leo
Aug 16	5:37P	Virgo
Sep 30	8:39P	Scorpio
Nov 15	10:40P	Scorpio
Dec 31	1:28A	Sagittarius

1973

Feb 13	4:31A	Capricorn
Mar 27	7:17A	Aquarius
May 9	11:03A	Pisces
Jun 21	1:56P	Aries
Aug 13	5:25P	Taurus
Oct 29	9:32P	Aries
Dec 25	1:13A	Taurus

1974

Feb 28	5:29A	Taurus
Apr 21	8:54A	Cancer
Jun 10	1:11P	Leo
Jul 28	4:21P	Virgo
Sep 13	7:26P	Libra
Oct 28	10:27P	Scorpio
Dec 11	12:13A	Sagittarius

1975

Jan 22	3:02P	Capricorn
Mar 4	5:44P	Aquarius
Apr 12	8:18P	Pisces
May 22	11:56A	Aries
Jul 2	2:37P	Taurus
Aug 15	5:31P	Gemini
Oct 17	9:43P	Cancer
Nov 25	11:17P	Gemini

MARS CHARTS
(EST & EDT)
♂

1976

Mar 19	6:46A	Cancer
May 17	11:39A	Leo
Jul 7	3:00P	Virgo
Aug 25	7:13P	Libra
Oct 8	9:10P	Scorpio
Nov 21	12:00A	Sagittarius

1979

Jan 21	3:42A	Aquarius
Feb 28	5:28A	Pisces
Apr 7	9:02A	Aries
May 17	11:36A	Taurus
Jun 27	2:18P	Gemini
Aug 9	5:07P	Cancer
Sep 24	8:12P	Leo
Nov 19	10:53P	Virgo

1977

Jan 2	1:46A	Capricorn
Feb 10	4:19A	Aquarius
Mar 21	6:43A	Pisces
Apr 28	10:23A	Aries
Jun 7	1:01P	Taurus
Jul 18	3:42P	Gemini
Sep 2	6:44P	Cancer
Oct 26	10:20P	Leo

1980

Mar 12	6:19A	Leo
May 5	10:52A	Virgo
Jul 11	3:16P	Libra
Aug 30	6:33P	Scorpio
Oct 12	9:26P	Sagittarius
Nov 22	11:08P	Capricorn
Dec 31	1:08A	Aquarius

1978

Jan 27	3:23A	Cancer
Apr 11	8:15A	Leo
Jun 14	2:31P	Virgo
Aug 5	4:52P	Libra
Sep 20	7:54P	Scorpio
Nov 1	10:47P	Sagittarius
Dec 13	12:25A	Capricorn

1981

Feb 7	4:08P	Pisces
Mar 17	9:41A	Aries
Apr 26	10:15A	Taurus
Jun 6	12:57A	Gemini
Jul 19	3:46P	Cancer
Sep 3	6:48P	Leo
Oct 21	10:01P	Virgo
Dec 16	1:42A	Libra

1982

Aug 4	4:48P	Scorpio
Sep 21	1:58P	Sagittarius
Oct 31	9:39P	Capricorn
Dec 11	12:17A	Aquarius

1983

Jan 18	2:51A	Pisces
Feb 26	8:21A	Aries
Apr 5	9:30P	Taurus
May 17	11:56A	Gemini
Jun 30	2:28P	Cancer
Aug 14	5:27P	Leo
Sep 29	11:30P	Virgo
Nov 18	10:49P	Libra

1984

Jan 12	2:22A	Scorpio
Aug 18	5:46P	Sagittarius
Oct 5	8:59P	Capricorn
Nov 15	10:40P	Aquarius
Dec 26	1:18A	Pisces

1985

Feb 3	3:52A	Aries
Mar 16	6:34A	Taurus
Apr 27	9:19A	Gemini
Jun 10	1:13P	Cancer
Jul 26	4:14P	Leo
Sep 11	7:19P	Virgo
Oct 27	9:25P	Libra
Dec 1	12:34A	Scorpio

1986

Feb 3	3:51A	Sagittarius
Mar 29	3:24A	Capricorn
Oct 9	12:00A	Aquarius
Nov 26	1:22A	Pisces

1987

Jan 9	2:08A	Aries
Feb 21	5:01A	Taurus
Apr 6	8:55A	Gemini
May 21	2:56A	Cancer
Jul 7	2:57P	Leo
Aug 23	6:03P	Virgo
Oct 8	9:08P	Libra
Nov 25	2:13A	Scorpio

1988

Jan 9	2:11A	Sagittarius
Feb 23	5:08P	Capricorn
Apr 7	9:01A	Aquarius
May 23	12:03P	Pisces
Jul 14	3:28P	Aries
Oct 23	10:10P	Taurus
Nov 1	9:45P	Gemini

1989

Jan 20	2:57A	Taurus
Mar 12	6:18A	Gemini
Apr 30	10:31A	Cancer
Jun 17	1:40P	Leo
Aug 4	4:50P	Virgo
Sep 20	7:55P	Libra
Nov 4	9:56P	Scorpio
Dec 19	12:50A	Sagittarius

January 1969		
Jan 1	12:00A	Gemini
Jan 2	11:00A	Cancer
Jan 4	11:00P	Leo
Jan 7	9:30A	Virgo
Jan 9	6:30P	Libra
Jan 12	12:30A	Scorpio
Jan 14	3:15A	Sagittarius
Jan 16	3:15A	Capricorn
Jan 18	3:00A	Aquarius
Jan 20	4:00A	Pisces
Jan 22	9:00A	Aries
Jan 24	5:00P	Taurus
Jan 27	5:00A	Gemini
Jan 29	5:30P	Cancer

March 1969		
Mar 2	11:00P	Virgo
Mar 5	6:30A	Libra
Mar 7	11:45A	Scorpio
Mar 9	3:45P	Sagittarius
Mar 11	6:30P	Capricorn
Mar 13	9:00P	Aquarius
Mar 15	11:40P	Pisces
Mar 18	4:00A	Aries
Mar 20	11:00A	Taurus
Mar 22	9:00P	Gemini
Mar 25	9:00A	Cancer
Mar 27	10:00P	Leo
Mar 30	8:00A	Virgo

February 1969		
Feb 1	5:45A	Leo
Feb 3	4:00P	Virgo
Feb 6	12:00A	Libra
Feb 8	6:30A	Scorpio
Feb 10	10:00A	Sagittarius
Feb 12	11:50A	Capricorn
Feb 14	1:15P	Aquarius
Feb 16	3:00P	Pisces
Feb 18	6:50P	Aries
Feb 21	2:00A	Taurus
Feb 23	12:45P	Gemini
Feb 26	1:00A	Cancer
Feb 28	1:00P	Leo

April 1969		
Apr 1	3:00P	Libra
Apr 3	7:30P	Scorpio
Apr 5	9:30P	Sagittarius
Apr 7	11:30P	Capricorn
Apr 10	3:30A	Aquarius
Apr 12	6:45A	Pisces
Apr 14	12:00P	Aries
Apr 16	7:45P	Taurus
Apr 19	5:45A	Gemini
Apr 21	5:00P	Cancer
Apr 24	6:00A	Leo
Apr 26	5:00P	Virgo
Apr 29	1:30A	Libra

MOON CHARTS
(EST & EDT)

🌙

May 1969

May 1	5:45A	Scorpio
May 3	7:00A	Sagittarius
May 5	8:00A	Capricorn
May 7	9:30A	Aquarius
May 9	1:00P	Pisces
May 11	7:00P	Aries
May 14	3:15A	Taurus
May 16	2:00A	Gemini
May 19	1:30A	Cancer
May 21	2:15P	Leo
May 24	2:00A	Virgo
May 26	11:00A	Libra
May 29	4:00P	Scorpio
May 30	5:00P	Sagittarius

June 1969

Jun 1	5:00P	Capricorn
Jun 3	5:00P	Aquarius
Jun 5	7:00P	Pisces
Jun 8	12:00A	Aries
Jun 10	9:00A	Taurus
Jun 12	7:55P	Gemini
Jun 15	7:55A	Cancer
Jun 17	8:30P	Leo
Jun 20	9:00A	Virgo
Jun 22	7:00P	Libra
Jun 25	1:30A	Scorpio
Jun 27	4:00A	Sagittarius
Jun 29	4:00A	Capricorn

July 1969

Jul 1	2:30A	Aquarius
Jul 3	3:30A	Pisces
Jul 5	7:30A	Aries
Jul 7	3:00P	Taurus
Jul 10	2:00A	Gemini
Jul 12	2:00P	Cancer
Jul 15	2:30A	Leo
Jul 17	2:30P	Virgo
Jul 20	1:00A	Libra
Jul 22	9:00A	Scorpio
Jul 24	12:40P	Sagittarius
Jul 26	1:40P	Capricorn
Jul 28	12:50P	Aquarius
Jul 30	1:00P	Pisces

August 1969

Aug 1	4:00P	Aries
Aug 3	10:00P	Taurus
Aug 6	7:50A	Gemini
Aug 8	8:00P	Cancer
Aug 11	8:30A	Leo
Aug 13	8:30P	Virgo
Aug 16	6:45A	Libra
Aug 18	3:00P	Scorpio
Aug 20	8:15P	Sagittarius
Aug 22	10:30P	Capricorn
Aug 24	11:30P	Aquarius
Aug 27	12:00A	Pisces
Aug 29	2:00A	Aries
Aug 31	7:00A	Taurus

September 1969

Sep 2	3:15P	Gemini
Sep 5	3:00A	Cancer
Sep 7	3:15P	Leo
Sep 10	3:00A	Virgo
Sep 12	1:00P	Libra
Sep 15	8:30A	Scorpio
Sep 17	1:30A	Sagittarius
Sep 19	5:00A	Capricorn
Sep 21	7:30A	Aquarius
Sep 23	9:30A	Pisces
Sep 25	11:30A	Aries
Sep 27	4:30A	Taurus
Sep 30	12:00A	Gemini

October 1969

Oct 2	11:00A	Cancer
Oct 4	11:30P	Leo
Oct 7	11:00A	Virgo
Oct 9	9:00P	Libra
Oct 12	3:00A	Scorpio
Oct 14	7:30A	Sagittarius
Oct 16	10:15A	Capricorn
Oct 18	1:00P	Aquarius
Oct 20	4:00P	Pisces
Oct 22	8:30P	Aries
Oct 25	1:30A	Taurus
Oct 27	8:00A	Gemini
Oct 29	7:00P	Cancer

November 1969

Nov 1	6:45A	Leo
Nov 3	7:00P	Virgo
Nov 6	5:00A	Libra
Nov 8	11:00A	Scorpio
Nov 10	3:30P	Sagittarius
Nov 12	4:00P	Capricorn
Nov 14	6:00P	Aquarius
Nov 16	9:00P	Pisces
Nov 19	1:15A	Aries
Nov 21	8:00A	Taurus
Nov 23	4:00P	Gemini
Nov 26	2:00A	Cancer
Nov 28	2:30P	Leo

December 1969

Dec 1	3:30A	Virgo
Dec 3	2:00P	Libra
Dec 5	9:30P	Scorpio
Dec 8	12:30A	Sagittarius
Dec 10	1:30A	Capricorn
Dec 12	1:30A	Aquarius
Dec 14	2:45A	Pisces
Dec 16	7:00A	Aries
Dec 18	1:30P	Taurus
Dec 20	10:30P	Gemini
Dec 23	9:00A	Cancer
Dec 25	9:30P	Leo
Dec 28	10:30A	Virgo
Dec 30	10:00P	Libra

January 1970		
Jan 2	7:00A	Scorpio
Jan 4	11:00A	Sagittarius
Jan 6	11:30A	Capricorn
Jan 8	11:30A	Aquarius
Jan 10	11:00A	Pisces
Jan 12	1:30P	Aries
Jan 14	7:00P	Taurus
Jan 17	5:00A	Gemini
Jan 19	3:45A	Cancer
Jan 22	4:30P	Leo
Jan 24	4:30P	Virgo
Jan 27	5:00A	Libra
Jan 29	2:45P	Scorpio
Jan 31	8:30P	Sagittarius

March 1970		
Mar 2	7:30A	Capricorn
Mar 4	9:00A	Aquarius
Mar 6	9:30A	Pisces
Mar 8	9:30A	Aries
Mar 10	1:00P	Taurus
Mar 12	7:00P	Gemini
Mar 15	4:00P	Cancer
Mar 17	5:00P	Leo
Mar 20	5:30P	Virgo
Mar 22	5:00P	Libra
Mar 25	2:00A	Scorpio
Mar 27	9:00A	Sagittarius
Mar 29	2:00P	Capricorn
Mar 31	5:00P	Aquarius

February 1970		
Feb 3	12:00A	Capricorn
Feb 5	12:00A	Aquarius
Feb 6	10:00P	Pisces
Feb 8	11:00P	Aries
Feb 11	3:00A	Taurus
Feb 13	11:45A	Gemini
Feb 15	9:30P	Cancer
Feb 18	10:00A	Leo
Feb 20	11:00P	Virgo
Feb 23	10:40A	Libra
Feb 25	8:00P	Scorpio
Feb 28	3:00A	Sagittarius

April 1970		
Apr 2	7:00P	Pisces
Apr 4	8:00P	Aries
Apr 6	11:00P	Taurus
Apr 9	4:00A	Gemini
Apr 11	12:30P	Taurus
Apr 14	12:00A	Leo
Apr 16	1:30P	Virgo
Apr 19	1:00A	Libra
Apr 21	9:00A	Scorpio
Apr 23	3:00P	Sagittarius
Apr 25	7:00P	Capricorn
Apr 28	12:00A	Aquarius
Apr 30	2:15A	Pisces

May 1970

May 2	5:00P	Aries
May 4	8:30A	Taurus
May 6	2:00P	Gemini
May 8	10:00P	Cancer
May 11	10:00A	Leo
May 13	10:30P	Virgo
May 16	10:00A	Libra
May 18	7:00P	Scorpio
May 21	12:00A	Sagittarius
May 23	3:45A	Capricorn
May 25	6:00A	Aquarius
May 27	8:00A	Pisces
May 29	12:00A	Aries
May 31	4:00P	Taurus

July 1970

Jul 2	2:00P	Cancer
Jul 5	12:30A	Leo
Jul 7	1:30P	Virgo
Jul 10	2:15P	Libra
Jul 12	12:15P	Scorpio
Jul 14	7:15P	Sagittarius
Jul 16	10:00P	Capricorn
Jul 18	10:30P	Aquarius
Jul 20	10:30P	Pisces
Jul 22	11:15A	Aries
Jul 25	3:30A	Taurus
Jul 27	10:00A	Gemini
Jul 29	7:30P	Cancer

June 1970

Jun 2	10:00P	Gemini
Jun 5	6:15A	Cancer
Jun 7	5:00P	Leo
Jun 10	6:00A	Virgo
Jun 12	6:15P	Libra
Jun 15	4:00A	Scorpio
Jun 19	9:30A	Sagittarius
Jun 21	12:30P	Aquarius
Jun 23	2:00P	Pisces
Jun 25	5:00P	Aquarius
Jun 27	9:00P	Taurus
Jun 30	4:15A	Gemini

August 1970

Aug 1	7:00A	Leo
Aug 3	7:30P	Virgo
Aug 6	9:00A	Libra
Aug 8	8:00P	Scorpio
Aug 11	4:00A	Sagittarius
Aug 13	9:00A	Capricorn
Aug 15	9:00P	Aquarius
Aug 17	9:00A	Pisces
Aug 19	9:00A	Aries
Aug 21	10:30A	Taurus
Aug 23	4:00P	Gemini
Aug 26	1:00A	Cancer
Aug 28	1:00P	Leo
Aug 31	2:00A	Virgo

September 1970

Sep 2	3:00P	Libra
Sep 5	2:00A	Scorpio
Sep 7	11:00A	Sagittarius
Sep 9	5:00P	Capricorn
Sep 11	7:00P	Aquarius
Sep 13	8:00P	Pisces
Sep 15	8:00A	Aries
Sep 18	8:00P	Taurus
Sep 20	12:00A	Gemini
Sep 22	8:00A	Cancer
Sep 24	7:30P	Leo
Sep 27	8:00A	Virgo
Sep 29	9:00P	Libra

November 1970

Nov 3	5:00A	Capricorn
Nov 5	7:30P	Aquarius
Nov 7	11:00A	Pisces
Nov 9	1:30P	Aries
Nov 11	4:00P	Taurus
Nov 13	7:00P	Gemini
Nov 16	12:45A	Cancer
Nov 18	10:00A	Leo
Nov 20	10:00P	Virgo
Nov 23	11:00A	Libra
Nov 25	9:00P	Scorpio
Nov 28	5:00A	Sagittarius
Nov 30	9:30A	Capricorn

October 1970

Oct 2	8:00A	Scorpio
Oct 4	4:30P	Sagittarius
Oct 6	11:00P	Capricorn
Oct 9	4:00A	Aquarius
Oct 11	6:00A	Pisces
Oct 13	6:00A	Aries
Oct 15	7:30A	Taurus
Oct 17	9:30P	Gemini
Oct 19	4:00P	Cancer
Oct 22	2:00A	Leo
Oct 24	3:00P	Virgo
Oct 27	3:00A	Libra
Oct 29	1:00P	Scorpio
Oct 31	9:00P	Sagittarius

December 1970

Dec 2	1:15P	Aquarius
Dec 4	5:00P	Pisces
Dec 6	8:00P	Aries
Dec 8	11:00P	Taurus
Dec 11	3:00A	Gemini
Dec 13	9:15A	Cancer
Dec 15	7:00P	Leo
Dec 18	6:30A	Virgo
Dec 21	7:00P	Libra
Dec 23	7:00A	Scorpio
Dec 25	2:00P	Sagittarius
Dec 27	6:30P	Capricorn
Dec 29	9:00P	Aquarius
Dec 31	11:00P	Pisces

January 1971

Jan 3	1:00A	Aries
Jan 5	5:00A	Taurus
Jan 7	10:30A	Gemini
Jan 9	5:15P	Cancer
Jan 12	2:45A	Leo
Jan 14	2:00P	Virgo
Jan 17	3:00A	Libra
Jan 19	3:00P	Scorpio
Jan 22	12:00A	Sagittarius
Jan 24	6:00A	Capricorn
Jan 26	7:15A	Aquarius
Jan 28	7:30A	Pisces
Jan 30	8:00A	Aries

February 1971

Feb 1	11:00A	Taurus
Feb 3	3:30P	Gemini
Feb 6	11:00A	Cancer
Feb 8	9:00A	Leo
Feb 10	9:00P	Virgo
Feb 13	10:00A	Libra
Feb 16	3:00P	Scorpio
Feb 18	8:30A	Sagittarius
Feb 20	3:00P	Capricorn
Feb 22	6:45P	Aquarius
Feb 24	8:15P	Pisces
Feb 26	6:45P	Aries
Feb 28	7:00A	Taurus

March 1971

Mar 2	9:30P	Gemini
Mar 5	5:15A	Cancer
Mar 7	3:00P	Leo
Mar 10	3:30P	Virgo
Mar 12	4:00P	Libra
Mar 15	4:45A	Scorpio
Mar 17	3:00P	Sagittarius
Mar 19	11:15P	Capricorn
Mar 22	6:00A	Aquarius
Mar 24	7:30A	Pisces
Mar 26	6:00A	Aries
Mar 28	5:00A	Taurus
Mar 30	6:45A	Gemini

April 1971

Apr 1	12:00A	Cancer
Apr 3	9:00P	Leo
Apr 6	9:00A	Virgo
Apr 8	10:30P	Libra
Apr 11	11:00A	Scorpio
Apr 13	10:00P	Sagittarius
Apr 16	6:45A	Capricorn
Apr 18	12:15P	Aquarius
Apr 20	4:00P	Pisces
Apr 22	5:00P	Aries
Apr 24	4:45P	Taurus
Apr 26	6:00P	Gemini
Apr 28	9:30P	Cancer

MOON CHARTS
(EST & EDT)

☾

May 1971

May 1	6:00A	Leo
May 3	5:00P	Virgo
May 6	6:00A	Libra
May 8	6:00P	Scorpio
May 11	4:00P	Sagittarius
May 13	12:00P	Capricorn
May 15	6:00P	Aquarius
May 17	10:15P	Pisces
May 20	1:00A	Aries
May 22	2:00A	Taurus
May 24	4:00A	Gemini
May 26	7:30A	Cancer
May 28	2:00P	Leo
May 31	1:00A	Virgo

June 1971

Jun 2	1:45P	Libra
Jun 5	1:45A	Scorpio
Jun 7	11:00A	Sagittarius
Jun 9	7:00P	Capricorn
Jun 12	12:00A	Aquarius
Jun 14	4:00A	Pisces
Jun 16	7:30A	Aries
Jun 18	9:00A	Taurus
Jun 20	12:00A	Gemini
Jun 22	4:00P	Cancer
Jun 24	11:30P	Leo
Jun 27	9:00A	Virgo
Jun 29	9:45P	Libra

July 1971

Jul 2	10:00A	Scorpio
Jul 4	8:00P	Sagittarius
Jul 7	3:30A	Capricorn
Jul 9	7:30A	Aquarius
Jul 11	10:00A	Pisces
Jul 13	12:30P	Aries
Jul 15	3:45P	Taurus
Jul 17	7:00P	Gemini
Jul 19	11:45P	Cancer
Jul 22	7:30A	Leo
Jul 24	5:30P	Virgo
Jul 27	5:15A	Libra
Jul 29	6:00P	Scorpio

August 1971

Aug 1	5:00A	Sagittarius
Aug 3	12:30P	Capricorn
Aug 5	4:30P	Aquarius
Aug 7	7:00P	Pisces
Aug 9	7:15P	Aries
Aug 11	9:00P	Taurus
Aug 14	12:00A	Gemini
Aug 16	6:00A	Cancer
Aug 18	2:00P	Leo
Aug 21	12:15A	Virgo
Aug 23	12:15P	Libra
Aug 26	1:30A	Scorpio
Aug 28	1:00P	Sagittarius
Aug 30	10:00P	Capricorn

MOON CHARTS
(EST & EDT)

☾

September 1971

Sep 2	3:00A	Aquarius
Sep 4	4:30A	Pisces
Sep 6	4:30A	Aries
Sep 8	4:30A	Taurus
Sep 10	7:00A	Gemini
Sep 12	11:00A	Cancer
Sep 15	8:00A	Leo
Sep 17	7:45A	Virgo
Sep 19	7:15P	Libra
Sep 22	7:45A	Scorpio
Sep 24	7:45P	Sagittarius
Sep 27	6:00A	Capricorn
Sep 29	12:00P	Aquarius

October 1971

Oct 1	3:00P	Pisces
Oct 3	3:15P	Aries
Oct 5	2:15P	Taurus
Oct 7	3:00P	Gemini
Oct 9	6:00P	Cancer
Oct 12	1:45A	Leo
Oct 14	12:00P	Virgo
Oct 17	1:00A	Libra
Oct 19	2:00P	Scorpio
Oct 22	2:00A	Sagittarius
Oct 24	12:00P	Capricorn
Oct 26	8:15P	Aquarius
Oct 29	12:30A	Pisces
Oct 31	1:00A	Aries

November 1971

Nov 2	1:00A	Taurus
Nov 4	1:00A	Gemini
Nov 6	2:30A	Cancer
Nov 8	8:00A	Leo
Nov 10	6:00P	Virgo
Nov 13	6:30A	Libra
Nov 15	6:45P	Scorpio
Nov 18	6:45A	Sagittarius
Nov 20	4:45P	Capricorn
Nov 23	1:00A	Aquarius
Nov 25	6:45A	Pisces
Nov 27	9:30A	Aries
Nov 29	11:00A	Taurus

December 1971

Dec 1	11:15A	Gemini
Dec 3	1:00P	Cancer
Dec 5	5:30P	Leo
Dec 8	1:30A	Virgo
Dec 10	1:00P	Libra
Dec 13	2:00A	Scorpio
Dec 15	1:30P	Sagittarius
Dec 17	11:00P	Capricorn
Dec 20	6:45A	Aquarius
Dec 22	12:00P	Pisces
Dec 24	4:00P	Aries
Dec 26	6:45P	Taurus
Dec 28	9:00P	Gemini
Dec 31	11:00P	Cancer

January 1972

Jan 2	3:00A	Leo
Jan 4	11:00A	Virgo
Jan 6	10:00P	Libra
Jan 9	10:30A	Scorpio
Jan 11	10:00P	Sagittarius
Jan 14	7:30A	Capricorn
Jan 16	2:00P	Aquarius
Jan 18	6:30P	Pisces
Jan 20	9:15P	Aries
Jan 23	12:30P	Taurus
Jan 25	3:00A	Gemini
Jan 27	7:15A	Cancer
Jan 29	12:30P	Leo

February 1972

Feb 1	8:00A	Virgo
Feb 3	6:00A	Libra
Feb 5	6:30P	Scorpio
Feb 8	6:30A	Sagittarius
Feb 10	5:00P	Capricorn
Feb 12	11:00P	Aquarius
Feb 15	3:00P	Pisces
Feb 17	5:00P	Aries
Feb 19	6:30P	Taurus
Feb 21	8:30P	Gemini
Feb 23	1:00P	Cancer
Feb 25	7:15P	Leo
Feb 28	4:00A	Virgo

March 1972

Mar 1	2:00P	Libra
Mar 4	2:00A	Scorpio
Mar 6	2:00P	Sagittarius
Mar 9	1:30A	Capricorn
Mar 11	9:15A	Aquarius
Mar 13	1:00P	Pisces
Mar 15	2:00P	Aries
Mar 17	2:00P	Taurus
Mar 19	3:00P	Gemini
Mar 21	6:30P	Cancer
Mar 24	1:00P	Leo
Mar 26	10:00A	Virgo
Mar 28	9:00P	Libra
Mar 30	8:30P	Scorpio

April 1972

Apr 2	10:00P	Sagittarius
Apr 5	9:00A	Capricorn
Apr 7	6:30P	Aquarius
Apr 9	11:30P	Pisces
Apr 12	1:00A	Aries
Apr 14	1:00A	Taurus
Apr 16	12:00A	Gemini
Apr 18	1:30A	Cancer
Apr 20	6:45A	Leo
Apr 22	4:00P	Virgo
Apr 25	4:00A	Libra
Apr 27	4:00P	Scorpio
Apr 30	4:00A	Sagittarius

May 1972

May 2	4:30P	Capricorn
May 5	2:00P	Aquarius
May 7	9:00A	Pisces
May 9	12:15P	Aries
May 11	12:15P	Taurus
May 13	12:00P	Gemini
May 15	12:00P	Cancer
May 17	4:00P	Leo
May 19	11:00P	Virgo
May 22	10:00A	Libra
May 24	10:00P	Scorpio
May 27	11:00A	Sagittarius
May 29	10:30P	Capricorn

July 1972

Jul 3	2:00A	Aries
Jul 5	5:00A	Taurus
Jul 7	7:30A	Gemini
Jul 9	8:45A	Cancer
Jul 11	11:00A	Leo
Jul 13	4:00P	Virgo
Jul 16	11:00A	Libra
Jul 18	12:30P	Scorpio
Jul 21	1:00A	Sagittarius
Jul 23	12:00P	Capricorn
Jul 26	9:00A	Aquarius
Jul 28	4:00A	Pisces
Jul 30	8:00A	Aries

June 1972

Jun 1	8:30A	Aquarius
Jun 3	4:00P	Pisces
Jun 5	9:00P	Aries
Jun 7	10:00P	Taurus
Jun 9	10:00P	Gemini
Jun 11	10:30P	Cancer
Jun 14	1:45A	Leo
Jun 16	7:30A	Virgo
Jun 18	5:00P	Libra
Jun 21	5:00A	Scorpio
Jun 23	5:30A	Sagittarius
Jun 26	5:00A	Capricorn
Jun 28	12:00P	Aquarius
Jun 30	9:00P	Pisces

August 1972

Aug 1	11:00A	Taurus
Aug 3	1:30P	Gemini
Aug 5	4:00P	Cancer
Aug 7	8:00A	Leo
Aug 10	2:00A	Virgo
Aug 12	9:30A	Libra
Aug 14	8:30P	Scorpio
Aug 17	9:00A	Sagittarius
Aug 19	9:00P	Capricorn
Aug 22	6:00A	Aquarius
Aug 24	11:00A	Pisces
Aug 26	2:15P	Aries
Aug 28	4:30P	Taurus
Aug 30	7:00P	Gemini

September 1972

Sep 1	10:00P	Cancer
Sep 4	3:00P	Leo
Sep 6	9:00A	Virgo
Sep 8	6:00P	Libra
Sep 11	4:00A	Scorpio
Sep 13	5:00P	Sagittarius
Sep 16	5:30A	Capricorn
Sep 18	2:00P	Aquarius
Sep 20	9:00P	Pisces
Sep 22	11:30P	Aries
Sep 25	12:00A	Taurus
Sep 27	1:00A	Gemini
Sep 29	4:00A	Cancer

November 1972

Nov 2	5:15A	Libra
Nov 4	5:00P	Scorpio
Nov 7	5:00A	Sagittarius
Nov 9	6:00P	Capricorn
Nov 12	6:00A	Aquarius
Nov 14	3:00P	Pisces
Nov 16	8:00P	Aries
Nov 18	9:00P	Taurus
Nov 20	8:00P	Gemini
Nov 22	7:30P	Cancer
Nov 24	9:00A	Leo
Nov 27	3:00A	Virgo
Nov 29	11:00A	Libra

October 1972

Oct 1	8:15A	Leo
Oct 3	4:00P	Virgo
Oct 6	1:00A	Libra
Oct 8	11:00A	Scorpio
Oct 11	12:00A	Sagittarius
Oct 13	1:00P	Capricorn
Oct 16	12:00A	Aquarius
Oct 18	7:00A	Pisces
Oct 20	10:00A	Aries
Oct 22	10:30A	Taurus
Oct 24	10:00A	Gemini
Oct 26	11:00A	Cancer
Oct 28	2:00P	Leo
Oct 30	8:00P	Virgo

December 1972

Dec 1	10:30P	Scorpio
Dec 4	11:30A	Sagittarius
Dec 7	12:30A	Capricorn
Dec 9	12:00P	Aquarius
Dec 11	9:00P	Pisces
Dec 14	4:00A	Aries
Dec 16	8:00A	Taurus
Dec 18	9:00A	Gemini
Dec 20	8:00A	Cancer
Dec 22	9:00A	Leo
Dec 24	11:00A	Virgo
Dec 26	6:30P	Libra
Dec 29	5:00A	Scorpio
Dec 31	6:15P	Sagittarius

January 1973

Jan 3	6:30A	Capricorn
Jan 5	5:30P	Aquarius
Jan 8	3:00A	Pisces
Jan 10	9:30A	Aries
Jan 12	2:45P	Taurus
Jan 14	4:00P	Gemini
Jan 16	5:30P	Cancer
Jan 18	6:45P	Leo
Jan 20	9:00P	Virgo
Jan 23	3:00P	Libra
Jan 25	1:00P	Scorpio
Jan 28	1:00A	Sagittarius
Jan 30	2:00P	Capricorn

March 1973

Mar 1	9:00A	Aquarius
Mar 3	5:30P	Pisces
Mar 5	10:30P	Aries
Mar 8	1:30A	Taurus
Mar 10	4:30A	Gemini
Mar 12	7:30P	Cancer
Mar 14	11:00A	Leo
Mar 16	3:30P	Virgo
Mar 18	10:00P	Libra
Mar 21	6:00A	Scorpio
Mar 23	5:45P	Sagittarius
Mar 26	6:30A	Capricorn
Mar 28	6:30P	Aquarius
Mar 31	3:00A	Pisces

February 1973

Feb 2	1:00A	Aquarius
Feb 4	9:00A	Pisces
Feb 6	3:00P	Aries
Feb 8	8:00P	Taurus
Feb 10	11:00P	Gemini
Feb 13	1:15A	Cancer
Feb 15	4:30A	Leo
Feb 17	7:30P	Virgo
Feb 19	1:00P	Libra
Feb 21	9:30P	Scorpio
Feb 24	9:30A	Sagittarius
Feb 28	10:00P	Capricorn

April 1973

Apr 2	8:00P	Aries
Apr 4	9:30A	Taurus
Apr 6	1:00A	Gemini
Apr 8	1:00P	Cancer
Apr 10	5:00P	Leo
Apr 12	9:30P	Virgo
Apr 15	5:00A	Libra
Apr 17	2:00P	Scorpio
Apr 20	1:00A	Sagittarius
Apr 22	2:00P	Capricorn
Apr 25	2:45A	Aquarius
Apr 27	12:30P	Pisces
Apr 29	7:00P	Aries

May 1973

May 1	9:00P	Taurus
May 3	9:00P	Gemini
May 5	9:15P	Cancer
May 8	12:00A	Leo
May 10	4:00A	Virgo
May 12	11:45A	Libra
May 14	9:00P	Scorpio
May 17	9:00A	Sagittarius
May 19	9:00P	Capricorn
May 22	10:00A	Aquarius
May 24	9:00P	Pisces
May 27	4:00A	Aries
May 29	7:30A	Taurus
May 31	8:00A	Gemini

June 1973

Jun 1	7:30A	Cancer
Jun 3	7:45A	Leo
Jun 6	11:00A	Virgo
Jun 8	5:00P	Libra
Jun 11	3:00A	Scorpio
Jun 13	3:00P	Sagittarius
Jun 16	4:00A	Capricorn
Jun 18	4:00P	Aquarius
Jun 20	3:30A	Pisces
Jun 23	12:00P	Aries
Jun 25	4:00P	Taurus
Jun 27	6:00P	Gemini
Jun 29	6:00P	Cancer

July 1973

Jul 1	6:00P	Leo
Jul 3	7:30P	Virgo
Jul 6	12:00A	Libra
Jul 8	9:00A	Scorpio
Jul 11	9:00P	Sagittarius
Jul 13	10:00A	Capricorn
Jul 15	10:00P	Aquarius
Jul 18	9:00A	Pisces
Jul 20	5:30P	Aries
Jul 23	12:00A	Taurus
Jul 25	3:00A	Gemini
Jul 27	4:00A	Cancer
Jul 29	4:00A	Leo
Jul 31	6:00A	Virgo

August 1973

Aug 2	9:00A	Libra
Aug 4	4:30P	Scorpio
Aug 7	4:00A	Sagittarius
Aug 9	5:00P	Capricorn
Aug 12	5:00A	Aquarius
Aug 14	3:30P	Pisces
Aug 16	11:30P	Aries
Aug 19	5:30A	Taurus
Aug 21	9:00A	Gemini
Aug 23	12:00P	Cancer
Aug 25	2:00P	Leo
Aug 27	3:00P	Virgo
Aug 29	7:00P	Libra

MOON CHARTS
(EST & EDT)

🌙

September 1973

Sep 1	1:30A	Scorpio
Sep 3	11:30P	Sagittarius
Sep 6	12:00A	Capricorn
Sep 8	12:00P	Aquarius
Sep 10	10:15P	Pisces
Sep 13	6:00A	Aries
Sep 15	11:00A	Taurus
Sep 17	2:30P	Gemini
Sep 19	4:00P	Cancer
Sep 21	9:00P	Leo
Sep 24	12:00A	Virgo
Sep 26	4:00P	Libra
Sep 28	10:00A	Scorpio
Sep 30	7:45P	Sagittarius

November 1973

Nov 1	4:15A	Aquarius
Nov 4	3:15P	Pisces
Nov 6	11:00P	Aries
Nov 9	3:00A	Taurus
Nov 11	5:00A	Gemini
Nov 13	5:45A	Cancer
Nov 15	7:15A	Leo
Nov 17	10:30A	Virgo
Nov 19	4:30P	Libra
Nov 22	12:30A	Scorpio
Nov 24	10:30P	Sagittarius
Nov 26	10:30P	Capricorn
Nov 29	11:00A	Aquarius

October 1973

Oct 3	8:15A	Capricorn
Oct 5	9:00P	Aquarius
Oct 8	7:15A	Pisces
Oct 10	2:00P	Aries
Oct 12	6:30P	Taurus
Oct 14	9:00P	Gemini
Oct 16	11:00P	Cancer
Oct 19	2:00P	Leo
Oct 21	6:30P	Virgo
Oct 23	11:30A	Libra
Oct 25	6:00P	Scorpio
Oct 28	4:00A	Sagittarius
Oct 30	3:00P	Capricorn

December 1973

Dec 1	11:30P	Pisces
Dec 4	9:00A	Aries
Dec 6	2:00P	Taurus
Dec 8	4:00P	Gemini
Dec 10	4:00P	Cancer
Dec 12	4:00P	Leo
Dec 14	6:00P	Virgo
Dec 16	9:30P	Libra
Dec 19	5:30A	Scorpio
Dec 21	4:45P	Sagittarius
Dec 24	5:00A	Capricorn
Dec 26	6:00P	Aquarius
Dec 29	6:00A	Pisces
Dec 31	5:00P	Aries

MOON CHARTS
(EST & EDT)

)

January 1974

Jan 2	11:15P	Taurus
Jan 5	3:00A	Gemini
Jan 7	3:15A	Cancer
Jan 9	2:30P	Leo
Jan 11	2:30P	Virgo
Jan 13	5:00A	Libra
Jan 15	12:00P	Scorpio
Jan 19	10:30P	Sagittarius
Jan 20	11:00A	Capricorn
Jan 23	12:00A	Aquarius
Jan 25	12:30P	Pisces
Jan 27	10:30P	Aries
Jan 30	6:45A	Taurus

February 1974

Feb 1	11:30A	Gemini
Feb 3	1:30P	Cancer
Feb 5	1:30P	Leo
Feb 7	1:30P	Virgo
Feb 9	3:00P	Libra
Feb 11	9:00P	Scorpio
Feb 14	5:00A	Sagittarius
Feb 16	5:00P	Capricorn
Feb 19	6:30A	Aquarius
Feb 21	6:30P	Pisces
Feb 24	4:00A	Aries
Feb 26	12:00P	Taurus
Feb 28	7:00P	Gemini

March 1974

Mar 2	9:30P	Cancer
Mar 5	12:00A	Leo
Mar 7	1:00A	Virgo
Mar 9	2:00A	Libra
Mar 11	6:00A	Scorpio
Mar 13	1:00P	Sagittarius
Mar 16	1:00A	Capricorn
Mar 18	2:00P	Aquarius
Mar 21	2:00A	Pisces
Mar 23	11:00A	Aries
Mar 25	6:00P	Taurus
Mar 27	11:00P	Gemini
Mar 30	4:00A	Cancer

April 1974

Apr 1	6:00A	Leo
Apr 3	9:00A	Virgo
Apr 5	11:30A	Libra
Apr 7	3:00P	Scorpio
Apr 9	10:45P	Sagittarius
Apr 12	9:00A	Capricorn
Apr 14	10:00P	Aquarius
Apr 17	10:00A	Pisces
Apr 20	9:45A	Aries
Apr 22	1:30A	Taurus
Apr 24	6:30A	Gemini
Apr 26	9:00A	Cancer
Apr 28	11:30A	Leo
Apr 30	4:00P	Virgo

227

May 1974

May 2	7:30P	Libra
May 5	12:15A	Scorpio
May 7	8:45A	Sagittarius
May 9	6:00P	Capricorn
May 12	6:45A	Aquarius
May 14	7:00P	Pisces
May 17	5:30A	Aries
May 19	12:00P	Taurus
May 21	4:00P	Gemini
May 23	6:00P	Cancer
May 25	7:30P	Leo
May 27	9:00P	Virgo
May 30	2:00A	Libra

July 1974

Jul 3	8:30A	Capricorn
Jul 5	9:00P	Aquarius
Jul 8	9:00A	Pisces
Jul 10	9:00P	Aries
Jul 13	6:00A	Taurus
Jul 15	12:00P	Gemini
Jul 17	2:00P	Cancer
Jul 19	2:00P	Leo
Jul 21	12:45P	Virgo
Jul 23	2:00P	Libra
Jul 25	7:00P	Scorpio
Jul 28	3:30A	Sagittarius
Jul 30	2:00P	Capricorn

June 1974

Jun 1	7:15A	Scorpio
Jun 3	3:30P	Sagittarius
Jun 6	2:00A	Capricorn
Jun 8	2:00P	Aquarius
Jun 11	3:00A	Pisces
Jun 13	2:00P	Aries
Jun 16	10:00A	Taurus
Jun 18	2:00A	Gemini
Jun 20	3:00A	Cancer
Jun 22	4:00A	Leo
Jun 24	4:00A	Virgo
Jun 26	7:00A	Libra
Jun 28	12:30P	Scorpio
Jun 30	9:45P	Sagittarius

August 1974

Aug 2	3:00A	Aquarius
Aug 4	4:00P	Pisces
Aug 7	3:30A	Aries
Aug 9	1:00P	Taurus
Aug 11	8:45P	Gemini
Aug 14	12:00A	Cancer
Aug 16	12:00A	Leo
Aug 18	12:00A	Virgo
Aug 20	12:00A	Libra
Aug 22	2:30A	Scorpio
Aug 24	10:00P	Sagittarius
Aug 27	8:30A	Capricorn
Aug 20	9:00A	Aquarius
Aug 31	9:30P	Pisces

September 1974

Sep 3	9:00A	Aries
Sep 5	7:00P	Taurus
Sep 8	2:00A	Gemini
Sep 10	7:30A	Cancer
Sep 12	10:00A	Leo
Sep 14	l0:00A	Virgo
Sep 16	10:00A	Libra
Sep 18	12:00P	Scorpio
Sep 20	6:00P	Sagittarius
Sep 23	3:45A	Capricorn
Sep 25	4:00P	Aquarius
Sep 28	4:30A	Pisces
Sep 30	3:30P	Aries

November 1974

Nov 1	2:00P	Gemini
Nov 3	7:00A	Cancer
Nov 5	10:15P	Leo
Nov 8	1:00A	Virgo
Nov 10	4:00A	Libra
Nov 12	7:30A	Scorpio
Nov 14	12:30P	Sagittarius
Nov 16	8:45P	Capricorn
Nov 19	7:45A	Aquarius
Nov 21	8:15P	Pisces
Nov 24	8:00A	Aries
Nov 26	4:00P	Taurus
Nov 28	10:30P	Gemini

October 1974

Oct 3	1:00A	Taurus
Oct 5	8:00P	Gemini
Oct 7	2:00P	Cancer
Oct 9	5:00P	Leo
Oct 11	7:00P	Virgo
Oct 13	8:15P	Libra
Oct 15	10:00P	Scorpio
Oct 18	3:45A	Sagittarius
Oct 20	12:00P	Capricorn
Oct 22	11:30P	Aquarius
Oct 25	12:00P	Pisces
Oct 27	11:00P	Aries
Oct 30	8:00A	Taurus

December 1974

Dec 1	1:00A	Cancer
Dec 3	3:00A	Leo
Dec 5	6:00A	Virgo
Dec 7	9:00A	Libra
Dec 9	1:00A	Scorpio
Dec 11	7:30P	Sagittarius
Dec 14	4:00A	Capricorn
Dec 16	3:00P	Aquarius
Dec 19	3:00A	Pisces
Dec 21	4:00P	Aries
Dec 24	2:00A	Taurus
Dec 26	8:00A	Gemini
Dec 28	11:00A	Cancer
Dec 30	12:00P	Leo

MOON CHARTS
(EST & EDT)
🌙

January 1975

Jan 1	1:00P	Virgo
Jan 3	3:00P	Libra
Jan 5	7:30P	Scorpio
Jan 8	2:00A	Sagittarius
Jan 10	11:00A	Capricorn
Jan 12	10:30P	Aquarius
Jan 15	10:45A	Pisces
Jan 17	11:00P	Aries
Jan 20	10:00A	Taurus
Jan 22	6:30P	Gemini
Jan 24	10:00P	Cancer
Jan 26	11:00P	Leo
Jan 28	10:30P	Virgo
Jan 30	10:30P	Libra

March 1975

Mar 1	9:30A	Scorpio
Mar 3	1:45P	Sagittarius
Mar 5	11:00P	Capricorn
Mar 8	10:30A	Aquarius
Mar 10	11:00P	Pisces
Mar 13	11:00A	Aries
Mar 15	11:00P	Taurus
Mar 18	8:30A	Gemini
Mar 20	4:00P	Cancer
Mar 22	7:30P	Leo
Mar 24	8:30P	Virgo
Mar 26	7:30P	Libra
Mar 28	8:00P	Scorpio
Mar 30	11:00P	Sagittarius

February 1975

Feb 2	1:00A	Scorpio
Feb 4	7:15A	Sagittarius
Feb 6	5:00P	Capricorn
Feb 9	4:00A	Aquarius
Feb 11	5:00P	Pisces
Feb 14	5:00A	Aries
Feb 16	5:00P	Taurus
Feb 19	2:45A	Gemini
Feb 21	8:00A	Cancer
Feb 23	9:45A	Leo
Feb 25	9:00A	Virgo
Feb 27	8:45A	Libra

April 1975

Apr 2	6:30A	Capricorn
Apr 4	5:00P	Aquarius
Apr 7	5:00A	Pisces
Apr 9	6:00P	Aries
Apr 12	5:00A	Taurus
Apr 14	2:00P	Gemini
Apr 16	9:30P	Cancer
Apr 19	2:00A	Leo
Apr 21	4:15A	Virgo
Apr 23	6:00A	Libra
Apr 25	6:30A	Scorpio
Apr 27	10:00P	Sagittarius
Apr 29	4:00P	Capricorn

MOON CHARTS
(EST & EDT)
☾

May 1975

May 2	1:30A	Aquarius
May 4	2:00P	Pisces
May 7	2:00A	Aries
May 9	1:00P	Taurus
May 11	9:30P	Gemini
May 14	4:00A	Cancer
May 16	8:30A	Leo
May 18	11:30A	Virgo
May 20	2:00P	Libra
May 22	4:15P	Scorpio
May 24	7:45P	Sagittarius
May 27	2:00A	Capricorn
May 29	10:00A	Aquarius
May 31	10:00P	Pisces

July 1975

Jul 3	6:30A	Taurus
Jul 5	3:00P	Gemini
Jul 7	7:30P	Cancer
Jul 9	10:30P	Leo
Jul 12	12:00A	Virgo
Jul 14	2:00A	Libra
Jul 16	4:15A	Scorpio
Jul 18	9:00A	Sagittarius
Jul 20	5:00P	Capricorn
Jul 23	2:00A	Aquarius
Jul 25	1:00P	Pisces
Jul 28	1:45A	Aries
Jul 30	2:00P	Taurus

June 1975

Jun 3	10:30A	Aries
Jun 5	9:30P	Taurus
Jun 8	6:00A	Gemini
Jun 10	10:00A	Cancer
Jun 12	2:00P	Leo
Jun 14	6:30P	Virgo
Jun 16	9:45P	Libra
Jun 18	10:00P	Scorpio
Jun 21	12:00A	Sagittarius
Jun 23	6:00P	Capricorn
Jun 25	6:00P	Aquarius
Jun 28	5:45A	Pisces
Jun 30	6:00P	Aries

August 1975

Aug 2	12:00A	Gemini
Aug 4	6:00A	Cancer
Aug 6	8:30A	Leo
Aug 8	9:00A	Virgo
Aug 10	9:00A	Libra
Aug 12	10:00A	Scorpio
Aug 14	2:00P	Sagittarius
Aug 16	10:00P	Capricorn
Aug 19	8:30A	Aquarius
Aug 21	7:30P	Pisces
Aug 24	8:15P	Aries
Aug 26	9:00P	Taurus
Aug 29	7:55A	Gemini
Aug 31	3:00P	Cancer

September 1975

Sep 2	7:00P	Leo
Sep 4	7:30P	Virgo
Sep 6	6:30P	Libra
Sep 8	7:00P	Scorpio
Sep 10	10:00P	Sagittarius
Sep 13	4:00A	Capricorn
Sep 15	2:00P	Aquarius
Sep 18	2:00A	Pisces
Sep 20	2:00P	Aries
Sep 23	3:00A	Taurus
Sep 25	2:00P	Gemini
Sep 27	11:00P	Cancer
Sep 30	4:00A	Leo

October 1975

Oct 2	6:00A	Virgo
Oct 4	5:30A	Libra
Oct 6	5:00A	Scorpio
Oct 8	7:00A	Sagittarius
Oct 10	11:45A	Capricorn
Oct 12	8:15P	Aquarius
Oct 15	7:45A	Pisces
Oct 17	8:30P	Aries
Oct 20	9:00A	Taurus
Oct 22	7:50P	Gemini
Oct 25	5:00A	Cancer
Oct 27	10:00A	Leo
Oct 29	1:30P	Virgo
Oct 31	3:00P	Libra

November 1975

Nov 2	3:00P	Scorpio
Nov 4	4:00P	Sagittarius
Nov 6	7:30P	Capricorn
Nov 9	3:00A	Aquarius
Nov 11	2:00P	Pisces
Nov 14	2:30A	Aries
Nov 16	3:00P	Taurus
Nov 19	1:00A	Gemini
Nov 21	8:00A	Cancer
Nov 23	4:00P	Leo
Nov 25	7:00P	Virgo
Nov 27	11:00P	Libra
Nov 30	1:00A	Scorpio

December 1975

Dec 2	3:00A	Sagittarius
Dec 4	7:00A	Capricorn
Dec 6	12:30P	Aquarius
Dec 8	10:00P	Pisces
Dec 11	10:00A	Aries
Dec 13	11:00P	Taurus
Dec 16	9:00A	Gemini
Dec 18	5:00P	Cancer
Dec 20	10:00P	Leo
Dec 23	1:00A	Virgo
Dec 25	4:00A	Libra
Dec 27	7:30A	Scorpio
Dec 29	11:00A	Sagittarius
Dec 31	3:00P	Capricorn

January 1976

Jan 2	9:00P	Aquarius
Jan 5	7:30A	Pisces
Jan 7	7:30P	Aries
Jan 10	6:30A	Taurus
Jan 12	7:30P	Gemini
Jan 15	2:00A	Cancer
Jan 17	6:00A	Leo
Jan 19	8:00A	Virgo
Jan 21	10:00A	Libra
Jan 23	1:00P	Scorpio
Jan 25	4:00P	Sagittarius
Jan 27	10:30P	Capricorn
Jan 30	7:00A	Aquarius

February 1976

Feb 1	3:00P	Pisces
Feb 4	2:30A	Aries
Feb 6	3:00P	Taurus
Feb 9	3:00A	Gemini
Feb 11	12:00A	Cancer
Feb 13	4:00P	Leo
Feb 15	7:00P	Virgo
Feb 17	7:30P	Libra
Feb 19	8:30P	Scorpio
Feb 21	10:30P	Sagittarius
Feb 24	4:00A	Capricorn
Feb 26	12:00P	Aquarius
Feb 28	10:00P	Pisces

March 1976

Mar 2	10:00A	Aries
Mar 4	10:30P	Taurus
Mar 7	11:00A	Gemini
Mar 9	9:00P	Cancer
Mar 12	3:00A	Leo
Mar 14	5:00A	Virgo
Mar 16	5:00A	Libra
Mar 18	4:45A	Scorpio
Mar 20	6:00A	Sagittarius
Mar 22	10:00A	Capricorn
Mar 24	5:00P	Aquarius
Mar 27	4:00A	Pisces
Mar 29	4:00P	Aries

April 1976

Apr 1	4:45A	Taurus
Apr 3	5:00P	Gemini
Apr 6	4:00A	Cancer
Apr 8	11:00A	Leo
Apr 10	3:00P	Virgo
Apr 12	4:00P	Libra
Apr 14	3:00P	Scorpio
Apr 16	3:00P	Sagittarius
Apr 18	6:00P	Capricorn
Apr 21	12:00A	Aquarius
Apr 23	9:00A	Pisces
Apr 25	10:00P	Aries
Apr 28	11:00A	Taurus
Apr 31	11:00P	Gemini

May 1976

May 3	11:00A	Cancer
May 5	6:00P	Leo
May 7	12:00P	Virgo
May 10	2:30A	Libra
May 12	3:00A	Scorpio
May 14	3:30A	Sagittarius
May 16	4:00A	Capricorn
May 18	9:00A	Aquarius
May 20	5:30P	Pisces
May 23	5:00A	Aries
May 25	6:15P	Taurus
May 28	6:30A	Gemini
May 30	5:00P	Cancer

June 1976

Jun 2	12:00A	Leo
Jun 4	6:30A	Virgo
Jun 6	10:00A	Libra
Jun 8	12:00P	Scorpio
Jun 9	1:00P	Sagittarius
Jun 12	2:30P	Capricorn
Jun 14	6:30P	Aquarius
Jun 17	2:00A	Pisces
Jun 19	1:00P	Aries
Jun 22	2:00P	Taurus
Jun 24	2:00P	Gemini
Jun 26	11:45P	Cancer
Jun 29	6:30A	Leo

July 1976

Jul 1	11:30P	Virgo
Jul 3	2:45P	Libra
Jul 5	6:30P	Scorpio
Jul 7	9:00P	Sagittarius
Jul 10	12:00A	Capricorn
Jul 12	4:00A	Aquarius
Jul 14	10:30A	Pisces
Jul 16	9:00P	Aries
Jul 19	9:00A	Taurus
Jul 21	9:30P	Gemini
Jul 24	7:45A	Cancer
Jul 26	2:00P	Leo
Jul 28	6:00P	Virgo
Jul 30	9:15P	Libra

August 1976

Aug 2	12:00A	Scorpio
Aug 4	3:00A	Sagittarius
Aug 6	7:00A	Capricorn
Aug 8	12:00P	Aquarius
Aug 10	7:00P	Pisces
Aug 13	5:00A	Aries
Aug 15	5:00P	Taurus
Aug 18	6:00A	Gemini
Aug 20	4:30P	Cancer
Aug 22	11:30P	Leo
Aug 25	2:30A	Virgo
Aug 27	4:15A	Libra
Aug 29	6:00A	Scorpio
Aug 31	8:30A	Sagittarius

September 1976

Sep 2	12:00P	Capricorn
Sep 4	6:00P	Aquarius
Sep 7	2:00A	Pisces
Sep 9	12:00P	Aries
Sep 12	12:00A	Taurus
Sep 14	2:00P	Gemini
Sep 17	1:00A	Cancer
Sep 19	9:00A	Leo
Sep 21	1:00P	Virgo
Sep 23	2:30P	Libra
Sep 25	2:30P	Scorpio
Sep 27	2:00P	Sagittarius
Sep 29	6:00A	Capricorn

November 1976

Nov 3	12:00A	Aries
Nov 5	12:45P	Taurus
Nov 8	1:30A	Gemini
Nov 10	1:30P	Cancer
Nov 12	11:15P	Leo
Nov 15	6:45A	Virgo
Nov 17	10:00A	Libra
Nov 19	11:30A	Scorpio
Nov 21	11:45P	Sagittarius
Nov 23	11:00A	Capricorn
Nov 25	1:45P	Aquarius
Nov 27	8:00P	Pisces
Nov 30	6:00A	Aries

October 1976

Oct 2	12:00A	Aquarius
Oct 4	8:30A	Pisces
Oct 6	7:00P	Aries
Oct 9	8:00A	Taurus
Oct 11	8:15P	Gemini
Oct 14	8:15A	Cancer
Oct 16	6:00P	Leo
Oct 18	11:00P	Virgo
Oct 21	1:00A	Libra
Oct 23	1:00A	Scorpio
Oct 25	12:30A	Sagittarius
Oct 27	2:00A	Capricorn
Oct 29	6:00A	Aquarius
Oct 31	1:00P	Pisces

December 1976

Dec 2	6:45P	Taurus
Dec 5	7:30P	Gemini
Dec 8	7:30A	Cancer
Dec 10	5:00A	Leo
Dec 12	1:00P	Virgo
Dec 14	6:00P	Libra
Dec 16	9:00P	Scorpio
Dec 18	9:30P	Sagittarius
Dec 20	9:40P	Capricorn
Dec 22	11:15P	Aquarius
Dec 25	5:00A	Pisces
Dec 27	2:00P	Aries
Dec 30	2:00A	Taurus

January 1977

Jan 1	3:00P	Gemini
Jan 4	2:00A	Cancer
Jan 6	11:00A	Leo
Jan 8	6:30P	Virgo
Jan 10	11:30P	Libra
Jan 13	4:00A	Scorpio
Jan 15	6:30A	Sagittarius
Jan 17	8:00A	Capricorn
Jan 19	10:00A	Aquarius
Jan 21	3:00P	Pisces
Jan 23	10:30P	Aries
Jan 26	10:00A	Taurus
Jan 28	11:00P	Gemini
Jan 31	10:30A	Cancer

March 1977

Mar 2	4:00A	Leo
Mar 4	10:00A	Virgo
Mar 6	1:00P	Libra
Mar 8	3:15P	Scorpio
Mar 10	5:45P	Sagittarius
Mar 12	8:30P	Capricorn
Mar 15	1:00P	Aquarius
Mar 17	7:15A	Pisces
Mar 19	3:30P	Aries
Mar 22	2:00A	Taurus
Mar 24	3:00P	Gemini
Mar 27	3:00A	Cancer
Mar 29	1:45P	Leo
Mar 31	8:30P	Virgo

February 1977

Feb 2	7:15P	Leo
Feb 5	1:00A	Virgo
Feb 7	5:30A	Libra
Feb 9	9:00A	Scorpio
Feb 11	12:00P	Sagittarius
Feb 13	3:00P	Capricorn
Feb 15	6:45P	Aquarius
Feb 17	11:30P	Pisces
Feb 20	7:30P	Aries
Feb 22	6:00P	Taurus
Feb 25	6:05A	Gemini
Feb 27	7:00P	Cancer

April 1977

Apr 2	11:00P	Libra
Apr 5	12:30A	Scorpio
Apr 7	1:00A	Sagittarius
Apr 9	3:00A	Capricorn
Apr 11	6:30A	Aquarius
Apr 13	1:00P	Pisces
Apr 15	10:00A	Aries
Apr 18	9:00A	Taurus
Apr 20	10:00P	Gemini
Apr 23	11:00A	Cancer
Apr 25	11:00P	Leo
Apr 28	7:00A	Virgo
Apr 30	11:00A	Libra

May 1977

May 2	12:00P	Scorpio
May 4	12:00P	Sagittarius
May 6	12:00P	Capricorn
May 8	2:00P	Aquarius
May 10	7:30P	Pisces
May 13	4:30A	Aries
May 15	4:00P	Taurus
May 18	5:00A	Gemini
May 20	6:00P	Cancer
May 23	5:00A	Leo
May 25	2:00P	Virgo
May 27	8:45P	Libra
May 29	10:30P	Scorpio
May 31	10:30P	Sagittarius

July 1977

Jul 2	9:00A	Aquarius
Jul 4	12:00P	Pisces
Jul 6	6:00P	Aries
Jul 9	5:00A	Taurus
Jul 11	5:30P	Gemini
Jul 14	5:30P	Cancer
Jul 16	5:00P	Leo
Jul 19	2:00A	Virgo
Jul 21	9:00P	Libra
Jul 23	2:00P	Scorpio
Jul 25	5:00P	Sagittarius
Jul 27	6:00P	Capricorn
Jul 29	7:00P	Aquarius
Jul 31	9:15P	Pisces

June 1977

Jun 2	10:00A	Capricorn
Jun 4	10:30P	Aquarius
Jun 7	3:00A	Pisces
Jun 9	11:00A	Aries
Jun 11	10:00P	Taurus
Jun 14	11:00A	Gemini
Jun 17	12:00A	Cancer
Jun 19	11:00A	Leo
Jun 21	8:30P	Virgo
Jun 24	3:30A	Libra
Jun 26	7:45A	Scorpio
Jun 28	8:00A	Sagittarius
Jun 30	9:00A	Capricorn

August 1977

Aug 3	3:00A	Aries
Aug 5	12:00P	Taurus
Aug 8	12:45A	Gemini
Aug 10	1:45P	Cancer
Aug 13	12:00A	Leo
Aug 15	8:30A	Virgo
Aug 17	3:00P	Libra
Aug 19	7:30P	Scorpio
Aug 21	10:30P	Sagittarius
Aug 24	2:00A	Capricorn
Aug 26	3:30A	Aquarius
Aug 28	7:00A	Pisces
Aug 30	12:00P	Aries

MOON CHARTS
(EST & EDT)
☾

September 1977

Sep 1	9:00P	Taurus
Sep 4	8:30A	Gemini
Sep 6	9:00P	Cancer
Sep 9	8:15A	Leo
Sep 11	4:30P	Virgo
Sep 13	10:00P	Libra
Sep 16	2:00A	Scorpio
Sep 18	4:00A	Sagittarius
Sep 20	7:00A	Capricorn
Sep 22	10:00A	Aquarius
Sep 24	2:00P	Pisces
Sep 26	10:45P	Aries
Sep 29	5:45A	Taurus

November 1977

Nov 3	12:00A	Leo
Nov 5	10:00P	Virgo
Nov 7	3:00P	Libra
Nov 9	8:00P	Scorpio
Nov 11	8:00P	Sagittarius
Nov 13	8:00P	Capricorn
Nov 15	9:00P	Aquarius
Nov 18	1:00A	Pisces
Nov 20	10:00P	Aries
Nov 22	6:00P	Taurus
Nov 25	6:00A	Gemini
Nov 27	6:30P	Cancer
Nov 30	6:50A	Leo

October 1977

Oct 1	4:30P	Gemini
Oct 4	5:00A	Cancer
Oct 6	5:00P	Leo
Oct 9	2:00A	Virgo
Oct 11	7:30A	Libra
Oct 13	10:00A	Scorpio
Oct 15	11:30A	Sagittarius
Oct 17	1:00P	Capricorn
Oct 19	3:00P	Aquarius
Oct 21	8:30P	Pisces
Oct 24	4:00A	Aries
Oct 26	1:00P	Taurus
Oct 29	12:00P	Gemini
Oct 31	11:30A	Cancer

December 1977

Dec 2	6:00P	Virgo
Dec 5	2:00A	Libra
Dec 7	6:30A	Scorpio
Dec 9	7:30P	Sagittarius
Dec 11	6:30A	Capricorn
Dec 13	6:00A	Aquarius
Dec 15	8:00A	Pisces
Dec 17	2:00P	Aries
Dec 20	12:00A	Taurus
Dec 22	12:00P	Gemini
Dec 25	12:45A	Cancer
Dec 27	1:00P	Leo
Dec 30	12:00A	Virgo

January 1978

Jan 1	9:30A	Libra
Jan 3	3:30P	Scorpio
Jan 5	6:00P	Sagittarius
Jan 7	6:00P	Capricorn
Jan 9	5:00P	Aquarius
Jan 11	6:00P	Pisces
Jan 13	10:00P	Aries
Jan 16	6:30A	Taurus
Jan 18	6:00P	Gemini
Jan 21	6:45A	Cancer
Jan 23	7:10P	Leo
Jan 26	6:00A	Virgo
Jan 28	3:00P	Libra
Jan 30	10:00P	Scorpio

March 1978

Mar 1	8:00A	Sagittarius
Mar 3	11:00A	Capricorn
Mar 5	1:00P	Aquarius
Mar 7	3:00P	Pisces
Mar 9	6:00P	Aries
Mar 12	12:30A	Taurus
Mar 14	10:00A	Gemini
Mar 16	10:00P	Cancer
Mar 19	10:30A	Leo
Mar 21	9:00P	Virgo
Mar 24	4:45A	Libra
Mar 26	10:00A	Scorpio
Mar 28	1:30P	Sagittarius
Mar 30	4:30P	Capricorn

February 1978

Feb 2	2:00A	Sagittarius
Feb 4	3:30A	Capricorn
Feb 6	4:00A	Aquarius
Feb 8	4:50A	Pisces
Feb 10	8:00A	Aries
Feb 12	3:00P	Taurus
Feb 15	1:30A	Gemini
Feb 17	2:00P	Cancer
Feb 20	2:00A	Leo
Feb 22	12:45P	Virgo
Feb 24	9:00P	Libra
Feb 27	3:30A	Scorpio

April 1978

Apr 1	7:00A	Aquarius
Apr 3	9:45P	Pisces
Apr 6	3:00A	Aries
Apr 8	9:00A	Taurus
Apr 10	6:30P	Gemini
Apr 13	6:00A	Cancer
Apr 15	6:00P	Leo
Apr 18	6:00A	Virgo
Apr 20	2:00P	Libra
Apr 22	6:45P	Scorpio
Apr 24	9:00P	Sagittarius
Apr 26	10:00P	Capricorn
Apr 29	12:30A	Aquarius

May 1978

May 1	5:00A	Pisces
May 3	10:30A	Aries
May 5	5:00P	Taurus
May 8	3:00A	Gemini
May 10	3:00P	Cancer
May 13	3:00A	Leo
May 15	3:00P	Virgo
May 18	12:00A	Libra
May 20	5:30A	Scorpio
May 22	7:30A	Sagittarius
May 24	7:45A	Capricorn
May 26	8:15A	Aquarius
May 28	10:30A	Pisces
May 30	4:00P	Aries

June 1978

Jun 2	12:00A	Taurus
Jun 4	10:00A	Gemini
Jun 6	9:30P	Cancer
Jun 9	10:00A	Leo
Jun 11	10:30P	Virgo
Jun 14	9:00A	Libra
Jun 16	3:00P	Scorpio
Jun 18	6:00P	Sagittarius
Jun 20	6:00P	Capricorn
Jun 22	5:00P	Aquarius
Jun 24	6:00P	Pisces
Jun 26	10:00P	Aries
Jun 29	5:30A	Taurus

July 1978

Jul 1	4:00P	Gemini
Jul 4	3:30A	Cancer
Jul 6	4:00P	Leo
Jul 9	5:00A	Virgo
Jul 11	4:00P	Libra
Jul 14	12:00A	Scorpio
Jul 16	4:00A	Sagittarius
Jul 18	4:30A	Capricorn
Jul 20	4:00A	Aquarius
Jul 22	3:00A	Pisces
Jul 24	6:00A	Aries
Jul 26	12:00P	Taurus
Jul 28	9:30P	Gemini
Jul 31	9:30P	Cancer

August 1978

Aug 2	10:00P	Leo
Aug 5	10:30A	Virgo
Aug 7	9:30P	Libra
Aug 10	6:00A	Scorpio
Aug 12	12:00P	Sagittarius
Aug 14	2:00P	Capricorn
Aug 16	2:00P	Aquarius
Aug 18	2:00P	Pisces
Aug 20	3:30P	Aries
Aug 22	8:00P	Taurus
Aug 25	5:00A	Gemini
Aug 27	4:00P	Cancer
Aug 30	5:00A	Leo

September 1978

Sep 1	5:00P	Virgo
Sep 4	3:00A	Libra
Sep 6	12:00P	Scorpio
Sep 8	6:00P	Sagittarius
Sep 10	9:00P	Capricorn
Sep 12	10:40P	Aquarius
Sep 15	12:00A	Pisces
Sep 17	2:00A	Aries
Sep 19	6:00A	Taurus
Sep 21	1:00P	Gemini
Sep 23	11:30P	Cancer
Sep 26	12:00P	Leo
Sep 29	12:00A	Virgo

November 1978

Nov 2	5:00A	Sagittarius
Nov 4	9:30A	Capricorn
Nov 6	10:00A	Aquarius
Nov 8	1:00P	Pisces
Nov 10	5:00P	Aries
Nov 12	11:00P	Taurus
Nov 15	6:00A	Gemini
Nov 17	3:15P	Cancer
Nov 20	3:00A	Leo
Nov 22	4:00P	Virgo
Nov 25	3:00A	Libra
Nov 27	10:30A	Scorpio
Nov 29	2:00P	Sagittarius

October 1978

Oct 1	10:00A	Libra
Oct 3	6:00P	Scorpio
Oct 6	10:30A	Sagittarius
Oct 8	2:30A	Capricorn
Oct 10	6:00A	Aquarius
Oct 12	8:15A	Pisces
Oct 14	11:00A	Aries
Oct 16	3:00P	Taurus
Oct 18	10:00P	Gemini
Oct 21	8:00A	Cancer
Oct 23	8:00P	Leo
Oct 26	8:30A	Virgo
Oct 28	7:00A	Libra
Oct 31	2:00A	Scorpio

December 1978

Dec 1	3:30P	Capricorn
Dec 3	4:30P	Aquarius
Dec 5	6:40P	Pisces
Dec 7	11:00P	Aries
Dec 10	5:00A	Taurus
Dec 12	1:00P	Gemini
Dec 14	11:00P	Cancer
Dec 17	11:15A	Leo
Dec 19	11:00P	Virgo
Dec 22	11:30A	Libra
Dec 24	8:30P	Scorpio
Dec 27	1:00A	Sagittarius
Dec 29	2:00A	Capricorn
Dec 31	2:00A	Aquarius

January 1979

Jan 2	2:00A	Pisces
Jan 4	5:00A	Aries
Jan 6	10:30A	Taurus
Jan 8	6:45P	Gemini
Jan 11	5:00A	Cancer
Jan 13	5:00P	Leo
Jan 16	6:00A	Virgo
Jan 18	6:45P	Libra
Jan 21	5:00A	Scorpio
Jan 23	11:00A	Sagittarius
Jan 25	1:00P	Capricorn
Jan 27	1:00P	Aquarius
Jan 29	12:30P	Pisces
Jan 31	1:00P	Aries

February 1979

Feb 2	5:00P	Taurus
Feb 5	1:00A	Gemini
Feb 7	11:00A	Cancer
Feb 9	11:30A	Leo
Feb 12	12:30P	Virgo
Feb 15	1:00A	Libra
Feb 17	11:00A	Scorpio
Feb 19	7:00A	Sagittarius
Feb 21	11:00P	Capricorn
Feb 24	12:00A	Aquarius
Feb 26	12:00A	Pisces
Feb 29	12:00A	Aries

March 1979

Mar 2	2:00A	Taurus
Mar 4	8:00P	Gemini
Mar 6	5:30P	Cancer
Mar 9	6:00A	Leo
Mar 11	6:45P	Virgo
Mar 14	6:30A	Libra
Mar 16	5:00P	Scorpio
Mar 19	1:00A	Sagittarius
Mar 21	6:00A	Capricorn
Mar 23	8:30A	Aquarius
Mar 25	10:00A	Pisces
Mar 27	10:30P	Aries
Mar 29	2:00P	Taurus
Mar 31	5:00P	Gemini

April 1979

Apr 3	1:30A	Cancer
Apr 5	1:00P	Leo
Apr 8	2:00A	Virgo
Apr 10	2:00P	Libra
Apr 12	11:00P	Scorpio
Apr 15	6:00A	Sagittarius
Apr 17	11:00A	Capricorn
Apr 19	3:00P	Aquarius
Apr 21	5:20P	Pisces
Apr 23	8:00P	Aries
Apr 26	10:30A	Taurus
Apr 28	3:00A	Gemini
Apr 30	11:30A	Cancer

May 1979

May 2	10:00P	Leo
May 5	11:00A	Virgo
May 7	11:00P	Libra
May 10	8:00A	Scorpio
May 12	2:00P	Sagittarius
May 14	6:30P	Capricorn
May 16	9:30P	Aquarius
May 19	12:00A	Pisces
May 21	3:30A	Aries
May 23	7:30A	Taurus
May 25	12:00P	Gemini
May 27	7:45P	Cancer
May 30	6:00A	Leo

July 1979

Jul 1	3:00P	Libra
Jul 4	2:00A	Scorpio
Jul 6	9:00A	Sagittarius
Jul 8	12:00P	Capricorn
Jul 10	1:00P	Aquarius
Jul 12	1:00P	Pisces
Jul 14	3:00P	Aries
Jul 16	7:00P	Taurus
Jul 19	1:00A	Gemini
Jul 21	10:00A	Cancer
Jul 23	9:00P	Taurus
Jul 26	9:30P	Gemini
Jul 28	10:00P	Libra
Jul 31	10:00A	Scorpio

June 1979

Jun 1	7:00P	Virgo
Jun 4	7:00A	Libra
Jun 6	5:00P	Scorpio
Jun 8	11:00P	Sagittarius
Jun 11	2:00A	Capricorn
Jun 13	4:00A	Aquarius
Jun 15	6:00A	Pisces
Jun 17	9:00A	Aries
Jun 19	1:30P	Taurus
Jun 21	7:30P	Gemini
Jun 24	3:00A	Cancer
Jun 26	2:00P	Leo
Jun 29	2:00A	Virgo

August 1979

Aug 2	6:00P	Sagittarius
Aug 4	10:00P	Capricorn
Aug 6	11:30P	Aquarius
Aug 8	11:00P	Pisces
Aug 10	11:00A	Aries
Aug 13	1:00A	Taurus
Aug 15	7:00A	Gemini
Aug 17	3:00P	Cancer
Aug 20	2:30A	Leo
Aug 22	3:00P	Virgo
Aug 25	4:00A	Libra
Aug 27	4:00P	Scorpio
Aug 30	2:00A	Sagittarius

September 1979

Sep 1	7:30A	Capricorn
Sep 3	10:00A	Aquarius
Sep 5	10:00A	Pisces
Sep 7	9:30A	Aries
Sep 9	10:00A	Taurus
Sep 11	2:00P	Gemini
Sep 13	9:30P	Cancer
Sep 16	8:15A	Leo
Sep 18	9:30P	Virgo
Sep 21	10:00A	Libra
Sep 23	10:00P	Scorpio
Sep 26	7:45A	Sagittarius
Sep 28	3:00P	Capricorn
Sep 30	7:00P	Aquarius

October 1979

Oct 2	8:30P	Pisces
Oct 4	8:30P	Aries
Oct 6	9:00P	Taurus
Oct 8	10:30P	Gemini
Oct 11	5:30A	Cancer
Oct 13	3:00P	Leo
Oct 16	4:00A	Virgo
Oct 18	5:00P	Libra
Oct 21	4:00A	Scorpio
Oct 23	1:00P	Sagittarius
Oct 25	8:15P	Capricorn
Oct 27	1:00A	Aquarius
Oct 30	8:30A	Pisces

November 1979

Nov 1	5:00A	Aries
Nov 3	6:00A	Taurus
Nov 5	9:00A	Gemini
Nov 7	1:00P	Cancer
Nov 9	10:00P	Leo
Nov 12	10:30A	Virgo
Nov 14	11:00P	Libra
Nov 17	10:30A	Scorpio
Nov 19	7:00P	Sagittarius
Nov 22	1:00A	Capricorn
Nov 24	5:30A	Aquarius
Nov 26	9:00A	Pisces
Nov 28	12:00P	Aries
Nov 30	3:00P	Taurus

December 1979

Dec 2	6:00P	Gemini
Dec 4	11:00P	Cancer
Dec 7	7:30A	Leo
Dec 9	6:30P	Virgo
Dec 12	7:30A	Libra
Dec 14	7:30P	Scorpio
Dec 17	3:30A	Sagittarius
Dec 19	9:00P	Capricorn
Dec 21	12:00P	Aquarius
Dec 23	3:00P	Pisces
Dec 25	5:30P	Aries
Dec 27	9:00P	Taurus
Dec 30	1:30A	Gemini

January 1980

Jan 1	8:30A	Cancer
Jan 3	4:00P	Leo
Jan 6	3:00A	Virgo
Jan 8	4:00P	Libra
Jan 11	4:00A	Scorpio
Jan 13	1:00P	Sagittarius
Jan 15	6:50P	Capricorn
Jan 17	9:00P	Aquarius
Jan 19	10:00P	Pisces
Jan 22	12:00A	Aries
Jan 24	2:30A	Taurus
Jan 26	7:15P	Gemini
Jan 28	2:00P	Cancer
Jan 30	11:00P	Leo

February 1980

Feb 2	11:00A	Virgo
Feb 4	11:00P	Libra
Feb 7	12:00P	Scorpio
Feb 9	10:00P	Sagittarius
Feb 12	5:00A	Capricorn
Feb 14	8:30A	Aquarius
Feb 16	9:00A	Pisces
Feb 18	9:00A	Aries
Feb 20	9:30A	Taurus
Feb 22	1:00P	Gemini
Feb 24	7:30P	Cancer
Feb 27	5:00A	Leo
Feb 29	5:00P	Virgo

March 1980

Mar 3	6:00A	Libra
Mar 5	6:30P	Scorpio
Mar 8	5:00A	Sagittarius
Mar 10	2:00P	Capricorn
Mar 12	7:00P	Aquarius
Mar 14	8:00P	Pisces
Mar 16	7:30P	Aries
Mar 18	7:15P	Taurus
Mar 20	9:00P	Gemini
Mar 23	2:00A	Cancer
Mar 25	11:00A	Leo
Mar 27	11:00P	Virgo
Mar 30	12:00P	Libra

April 1980

Apr 2	12:30a	Scorpio
Apr 4	12:00P	Sagittarius
Apr 6	9:00P	Capricorn
Apr 9	3:00A	Aquarius
Apr 11	6:00A	Pisces
Apr 13	6:45A	Aries
Apr 15	6:15A	Taurus
Apr 17	6:15A	Gemini
Apr 19	10:30A	Cancer
Apr 21	6:00P	Leo
Apr 24	5:00A	Virgo
Apr 26	6:00P	Libra
Apr 29	7:30A	Scorpio

May 1980

May 1	6:30P	Sagittarius
May 4	3:00A	Capricorn
May 6	10:00A	Aquarius
May 8	2:30P	Pisces
May 10	4:30P	Aries
May 12	5:30P	Taurus
May 14	6:00P	Gemini
May 16	9:00P	Cancer
May 19	3:30A	Leo
May 21	2:00P	Virgo
May 24	2:00A	Libra
May 26	3:00P	Scorpio
May 29	1:00A	Sagittarius
May 31	9:00A	Capricorn

July 1980

Jul 2	2:00A	Pisces
Jul 4	4:00A	Aries
Jul 6	7:30A	Taurus
Jul 8	10:30A	Gemini
Jul 10	3:00P	Cancer
Jul 12	3:00P	Leo
Jul 15	6:00A	Virgo
Jul 17	6:00P	Libra
Jul 20	6:30A	Scorpio
Jul 22	6:30P	Sagittarius
Jul 25	2:00A	Capricorn
Jul 27	6:30A	Aquarius
Jul 29	9:15A	Pisces
Jul 31	11:00A	Aries

June 1980

Jun 2	3:30P	Aquarius
Jun 4	8:15P	Pisces
Jun 6	11:00P	Aries
Jun 9	2:00A	Taurus
Jun 11	3:00A	Gemini
Jun 13	6:30A	Cancer
Jun 15	12:30P	Leo
Jun 17	10:00P	Virgo
Jun 20	10:00A	Libra
Jun 22	10:30P	Scorpio
Jun 25	9:00A	Sagittarius
Jun 27	5:00P	Capricorn
Jun 29	10:00P	Aquarius

August 1980

Aug 2	1:00P	Taurus
Aug 4	4:00P	Gemini
Aug 6	9:00P	Cancer
Aug 9	4:15A	Leo
Aug 11	2:00P	Virgo
Aug 14	1:30A	Libra
Aug 16	2:00P	Scorpio
Aug 19	2:00A	Sagittarius
Aug 21	11:00A	Capricorn
Aug 23	4:00P	Aquarius
Aug 25	6:30P	Pisces
Aug 27	7:00P	Aries
Aug 29	7:30P	Taurus
Aug 31	10:00P	Gemini

September 1980

Sep 3	3:00A	Cancer
Sep 5	10:00A	Leo
Sep 7	8:30P	Virgo
Sep 10	8:30A	Libra
Sep 12	9:00P	Scorpio
Sep 15	9:30A	Sagittarius
Sep 17	7:45P	Capricorn
Sep 20	2:00A	Aquarius
Sep 22	5:30A	Pisces
Sep 24	5:30A	Aries
Sep 26	4:30A	Taurus
Sep 28	5:00A	Gemini
Sep 30	8:45A	Cancer

November 1980

Nov 1	7:30A	Virgo
Nov 3	7:30P	Libra
Nov 6	8:00A	Scorpio
Nov 8	8:00P	Sagittarius
Nov 11	7:15A	Capricorn
Nov 13	4:00P	Aquarius
Nov 15	10:00P	Pisces
Nov 18	1:00A	Aries
Nov 20	1:30A	Taurus
Nov 22	1:00A	Gemini
Nov 24	2:00A	Cancer
Nov 26	6:30A	Leo
Nov 28	3:00P	Virgo

October 1980

Oct 2	4:00P	Leo
Oct 5	3:00A	Virgo
Oct 7	2:00P	Libra
Oct 10	3:30A	Scorpio
Oct 12	4:00P	Sagittarius
Oct 17	10:30A	Aquarius
Oct 19	3:30P	Pisces
Oct 21	4:30P	Aries
Oct 23	4:00P	Taurus
Oct 25	3:00P	Gemini
Oct 27	5:00P	Cancer
Oct 29	10:30P	Leo

December 1980

Dec 1	2:30A	Libra
Dec 3	3:00P	Scorpio
Dec 6	3:00A	Sagittarius
Dec 8	1:00P	Capricorn
Dec 10	9:00P	Aquarius
Dec 13	4:00A	Pisces
Dec 15	8:30A	Aries
Dec 17	10:00A	Taurus
Dec 19	11:30A	Gemini
Dec 21	1:00P	Cancer
Dec 23	4:30P	Leo
Dec 25	11:00P	Virgo
Dec 28	9:30P	Libra
Dec 30	11:00P	Scorpio

January 1981

Jan 2	11:00A	Sagittarius
Jan 4	9:00P	Capricorn
Jan 7	4:00A	Aquarius
Jan 9	9:15A	Pisces
Jan 11	1:30P	Aries
Jan 13	5:00P	Taurus
Jan 15	7:15P	Gemini
Jan 17	10:00P	Cancer
Jan 20	2:00A	Leo
Jan 22	9:00P	Virgo
Jan 24	6:45P	Libra
Jan 27	6:45A	Scorpio
Jan 29	7:15P	Sagittarius

March 1981

Mar 2	11:00P	Aquarius
Mar 5	3:00A	Pisces
Mar 7	5:00A	Aries
Mar 9	5:00A	Taurus
Mar 11	6:50A	Gemini
Mar 13	9:45A	Cancer
Mar 15	4:00P	Leo
Mar 18	12:00P	Virgo
Mar 20	11:00A	Libra
Mar 22	10:00P	Scorpio
Mar 25	11:00A	Sagittarius
Mar 27	11:00P	Capricorn
Mar 30	8:00A	Aquarius

February 1981

Feb 1	5:30A	Capricorn
Feb 3	1:00P	Aquarius
Feb 5	5:15P	Pisces
Feb 7	8:00P	Aries
Feb 9	10:00P	Taurus
Feb 12	1:00A	Gemini
Feb 14	5:00A	Cancer
Feb 16	10:30A	Leo
Feb 18	5:30P	Virgo
Feb 21	3:00A	Libra
Feb 23	3:00P	Scorpio
Feb 26	3:30A	Sagittarius
Feb 28	3:00P	Capricorn

April 1981

Apr 1	1:30P	Pisces
Apr 3	3:00P	Aries
Apr 5	3:00P	Taurus
Apr 7	3:00P	Gemini
Apr 9	4:00P	Cancer
Apr 11	9:30P	Leo
Apr 14	6:00A	Virgo
Apr 16	5:00P	Libra
Apr 19	5:00A	Scorpio
Apr 21	5:00P	Sagittarius
Apr 24	5:30A	Capricorn
Apr 26	5:00P	Aquarius
Apr 29	12:00A	Pisces

May 1981

May 1	3:00A	Aries
May 3	3:00A	Taurus
May 5	2:00A	Gemini
May 7	2:00A	Cancer
May 9	6:00A	Leo
May 11	1:00P	Virgo
May 13	11:30P	Libra
May 16	12:00P	Scorpio
May 19	12:00A	Sagittarius
May 21	12:00P	Capricorn
May 23	11:00P	Aquarius
May 26	7:00A	Pisces
May 28	11:30A	Aries
May 30	12:40P	Taurus

July 1981

Jul 3	12:30A	Leo
Jul 5	5:00A	Virgo
Jul 7	2:00P	Libra
Jul 10	1:00A	Scorpio
Jul 12	2:00P	Sagittarius
Jul 15	1:30A	Capricorn
Jul 17	10:30A	Aquarius
Jul 19	6:30P	Pisces
Jul 22	12:00A	Aries
Jul 24	3:00A	Taurus
Jul 26	6:00A	Gemini
Jul 28	7:45A	Cancer
Jul 30	10:00A	Leo

June 1981

Jun 1	1:00P	Gemini
Jun 3	1:00P	Cancer
Jun 5	2:30P	Leo
Jun 7	8:30P	Virgo
Jun 10	6:00A	Libra
Jun 12	6:00P	Scorpio
Jun 15	6:30A	Sagittarius
Jun 17	6:30P	Capricorn
Jun 20	5:00A	Aquarius
Jun 22	1:00P	Pisces
Jun 24	6:00P	Aries
Jun 26	9:00P	Taurus
Jun 28	10:00P	Gemini
Jun 30	10:30P	Cancer

August 1981

Aug 1	3:00P	Virgo
Aug 3	10:00P	Libra
Aug 6	9:00A	Scorpio
Aug 8	9:15A	Sagittarius
Aug 11	9:00A	Capricorn
Aug 13	7:00P	Aquarius
Aug 16	2:00A	Pisces
Aug 18	5:45A	Aries
Aug 20	7:45P	Taurus
Aug 22	10:30A	Gemini
Aug 24	2:00P	Cancer
Aug 26	6:00P	Leo
Aug 28	11:00P	Virgo
Aug 31	7:30A	Libra

MOON CHARTS
(EST & EDT)

☾

September 1981

Sep 2	5:00P	Scorpio
Sep 5	5:30A	Sagittarius
Sep 7	6:00P	Capricorn
Sep 10	4:00A	Aquarius
Sep 12	10:00A	Pisces
Sep 14	2:00P	Aries
Sep 16	4:00P	Taurus
Sep 18	5:00P	Gemini
Sep 20	7:45P	Cancer
Sep 23	12:00A	Leo
Sep 25	6:30A	Virgo
Sep 27	3:00P	Libra
Sep 30	1:00A	Scorpio

October 1981

Oct 2	1:00P	Sagittarius
Oct 5	2:00A	Capricorn
Oct 7	1:00P	Aquarius
Oct 9	8:30P	Pisces
Oct 12	12:00A	Aries
Oct 14	1:00A	Taurus
Oct 16	12:30A	Gemini
Oct 18	2:00A	Cancer
Oct 20	6:00A	Leo
Oct 22	12:00P	Virgo
Oct 24	9:00P	Libra
Oct 27	6:45A	Scorpio
Oct 29	6:50P	Sagittarius

November 1981

Nov 1	7:45P	Capricorn
Nov 3	8:00P	Aquarius
Nov 6	5:00A	Pisces
Nov 8	9:00A	Aries
Nov 10	10:15A	Taurus
Nov 12	9:30A	Gemini
Nov 14	9:30A	Cancer
Nov 16	11:15A	Leo
Nov 18	5:00P	Virgo
Nov 21	2:00A	Libra
Nov 23	1:00P	Scorpio
Nov 26	1:00A	Sagittarius
Nov 28	2:00P	Capricorn

December 1981

Dec 1	2:00A	Aquarius
Dec 3	12:00P	Pisces
Dec 5	6:50P	Aries
Dec 7	9:15P	Taurus
Dec 9	9:00P	Gemini
Dec 11	8:30P	Cancer
Dec 13	9:00P	Leo
Dec 16	1:00A	Virgo
Dec 18	8:00A	Libra
Dec 20	6:45P	Scorpio
Dec 23	7:15A	Sagittarius
Dec 25	8:00P	Capricorn
Dec 28	8:00A	Aquarius
Dec 30	6:00P	Pisces

January 1982

Jan 2	1:30A	Aries
Jan 4	6:00A	Taurus
Jan 6	8:00A	Gemini
Jan 8	8:00A	Cancer
Jan 10	8:30A	Leo
Jan 12	10:30A	Virgo
Jan 14	4:00P	Libra
Jan 17	2:00A	Scorpio
Jan 19	2:00P	Sagittarius
Jan 22	3:00A	Capricorn
Jan 24	3:00P	Aquarius
Jan 26	11:30P	Pisces
Jan 29	7:00A	Aries
Jan 31	12:00P	Taurus

March 1982

Mar 1	8:30P	Gemini
Mar 3	11:30P	Cancer
Mar 6	3:00A	Leo
Mar 8	6:30A	Virgo
Mar 10	12:00P	Libra
Mar 12	7:15P	Scorpio
Mar 15	6:00A	Sagittarius
Mar 17	6:45P	Capricorn
Mar 20	6:45A	Aquarius
Mar 22	4:00P	Pisces
Mar 24	9:00P	Aries
Mar 27	1:00A	Taurus
Mar 29	3:00A	Gemini
Mar 31	5:00A	Cancer

February 1982

Feb 2	3:00P	Gemini
Feb 4	5:00P	Cancer
Feb 6	7:00P	Leo
Feb 8	9:00P	Virgo
Feb 11	2:00A	Libra
Feb 13	10:00A	Scorpio
Feb 15	10:00P	Sagittarius
Feb 18	11:00A	Capricorn
Feb 20	10:00P	Aquarius
Feb 23	7:10P	Pisces
Feb 25	1:00P	Aries
Feb 27	5:30P	Taurus

April 1982

Apr 2	8:30P	Leo
Apr 4	1:00P	Virgo
Apr 6	7:30P	Libra
Apr 9	3:30A	Scorpio
Apr 11	2:00P	Sagittarius
Apr 14	3:00A	Capricorn
Apr 16	3:00P	Aquarius
Apr 19	1:00A	Pisces
Apr 21	7:15A	Aries
Apr 23	9:30A	Taurus
Apr 25	12:00P	Gemini
Apr 27	1:00P	Cancer
Apr 29	3:00P	Leo

May 1982

May 1	7:45P	Virgo
May 4	3:00A	Libra
May 6	11:30A	Scorpio
May 8	10:00P	Sagittarius
May 11	11:00A	Capricorn
May 14	12:00A	Aquarius
May 16	11:00A	Pisces
May 18	6:00A	Aries
May 20	9:00P	Taurus
May 22	10:00P	Gemini
May 24	10:00P	Cancer
May 26	10:00P	Leo
May 29	2:00A	Virgo
May 31	8:10A	Libra

June 1982

Jun 2	5:00P	Scorpio
Jun 5	5:00A	Sagittarius
Jun 7	5:00P	Capricorn
Jun 10	6:00A	Aquarius
Jun 12	6:00P	Pisces
Jun 15	2:00A	Aries
Jun 17	7:00A	Taurus
Jun 19	8:15A	Gemini
Jun 21	8:15A	Cancer
Jun 23	8:00A	Leo
Jun 25	9:15A	Virgo
Jun 27	2:00P	Libra
Jun 29	11:30P	Scorpio

July 1982

Jul 2	11:00A	Sagittarius
Jul 4	11:30P	Capricorn
Jul 7	12:00P	Aquarius
Jul 9	11:00P	Pisces
Jul 12	8:30A	Aries
Jul 14	3:00P	Taurus
Jul 16	6:00P	Gemini
Jul 18	7:00P	Cancer
Jul 20	6:30P	Leo
Jul 22	7:30P	Virgo
Jul 24	10:30P	Libra
Jul 27	6:00A	Scorpio
Jul 29	5:00P	Sagittarius

August 1982

Aug 1	6:00A	Capricorn
Aug 3	6:00P	Aquarius
Aug 6	5:00A	Pisces
Aug 8	2:00P	Aries
Aug 10	9:00P	Taurus
Aug 13	1:00A	Gemini
Aug 15	4:00A	Cancer
Aug 17	4:15A	Leo
Aug 19	6:00A	Virgo
Aug 21	8:30A	Libra
Aug 23	2:00P	Scorpio
Aug 26	12:00A	Sagittarius
Aug 28	1:00P	Capricorn
Aug 31	1:00A	Aquarius

MOON CHARTS
(EST & EDT)

🌙

September 1982

Sep 2	12:00P	Pisces
Sep 4	8:30P	Aries
Sep 7	2:00A	Taurus
Sep 9	7:00A	Gemini
Sep 11	10:00A	Cancer
Sep 13	4:15P	Leo
Sep 15	3:00P	Virgo
Sep 17	6:00P	Libra
Sep 20	12:00A	Scorpio
Sep 22	8:30A	Sagittarius
Sep 24	8:30P	Capricorn
Sep 27	9:00A	Aquarius
Sep 29	8:15P	Pisces

October 1982

Oct 2	4:00A	Aries
Oct 4	9:00A	Taurus
Oct 6	12:30P	Gemini
Oct 8	3:30P	Cancer
Oct 10	7:00P	Leo
Oct 12	10:00P	Virgo
Oct 15	2:00A	Libra
Oct 17	8:30A	Scorpio
Oct 19	5:00P	Sagittarius
Oct 22	5:00A	Capricorn
Oct 24	6:00P	Aquarius
Oct 27	5:00A	Pisces
Oct 29	1:30P	Aries
Oct 31	5:00P	Taurus

November 1982

Nov 3	7:30A	Gemini
Nov 5	9:00A	Cancer
Nov 6	11:00P	Leo
Nov 9	3:00A	Virgo
Nov 11	8:00A	Libra
Nov 13	3:00P	Scorpio
Nov 16	12:00A	Sagittarius
Nov 18	11:00A	Capricorn
Nov 21	12:45A	Aquarius
Nov 23	1:00P	Pisces
Nov 25	10:00P	Aries
Nov 28	3:00A	Taurus
Nov 30	5:30A	Gemini

December 1982

Dec 2	6:00A	Cancer
Dec 4	6:30A	Leo
Dec 6	8:30P	Virgo
Dec 8	1:00P	Libra
Dec 10	9:00P	Scorpio
Dec 13	6:30A	Sagittarius
Dec 15	6:15P	Capricorn
Dec 18	7:15A	Aquarius
Dec 20	8:00P	Pisces
Dec 23	6:30A	Aries
Dec 25	1:30P	Taurus
Dec 27	5:00P	Gemini
Dec 29	5:00P	Cancer
Dec 31	4:30P	Leo

January 1983

Jan 2	5:00P	Virgo
Jan 4	8:00P	Libra
Jan 7	2:30A	Scorpio
Jan 9	12:30A	Sagittarius
Jan 12	1:00A	Capricorn
Jan 14	1:00P	Aquarius
Jan 17	2:00A	Pisces
Jan 19	1:00P	Aries
Jan 21	9:00P	Taurus
Jan 24	3:00A	Gemini
Jan 26	4:00A	Cancer
Jan 28	4:00A	Leo
Jan 30	4:00A	Virgo

March 1983

Mar 2	6:45P	Scorpio
Mar 5	2:30A	Sagittarius
Mar 7	1:30P	Capricorn
Mar 10	3:00A	Aquarius
Mar 12	3:00P	Pisces
Mar 15	1:00A	Aries
Mar 17	9:00P	Taurus
Mar 19	3:00P	Gemini
Mar 21	8:00P	Cancer
Mar 23	11:00P	Leo
Mar 25	11:45P	Virgo
Mar 28	1:30A	Libra
Mar 30	5:00A	Scorpio

February 1983

Feb 1	5:00A	Libra
Feb 3	9:30A	Scorpio
Feb 5	6:30P	Sagittarius
Feb 8	6:45P	Capricorn
Feb 10	8:00P	Aquarius
Feb 13	8:00A	Pisces
Feb 15	6:45P	Aries
Feb 18	3:30A	Taurus
Feb 20	10:00A	Gemini
Feb 22	1:00P	Cancer
Feb 24	3:00P	Leo
Feb 26	3:00P	Virgo
Feb 28	3:30P	Libra

April 1983

Apr 1	12:00P	Sagittarius
Apr 3	8:30P	Capricorn
Apr 6	11:00A	Aquarius
Apr 8	11:30P	Pisces
Apr 11	9:00A	Aries
Apr 13	5:00P	Taurus
Apr 15	10:00P	Gemini
Apr 18	2:00A	Cancer
Apr 20	5:00A	Leo
Apr 22	8:15A	Virgo
Apr 24	10:30A	Libra
Apr 26	3:00P	Scorpio
Apr 28	9:30P	Sagittarius

May 1983

May 1	7:00A	Capricorn
May 3	7:00P	Aquarius
May 6	8:00A	Pisces
May 8	6:00P	Aries
May 11	2:00A	Taurus
May 13	6:00P	Gemini
May 15	8:45A	Cancer
May 17	10:30A	Leo
May 19	1:45P	Virgo
May 21	5:00P	Libra
May 23	10:00P	Scorpio
May 26	5:30A	Sagittarius
May 28	3:00P	Capricorn
May 31	3:00A	Aquarius

July 1983

Jul 2	11:00A	Aries
Jul 4	8:00P	Taurus
Jul 7	2:00A	Gemini
Jul 9	4:00A	Cancer
Jul 11	4:00A	Leo
Jul 13	4:00A	Virgo
Jul 15	5:00A	Libra
Jul 17	10:00A	Scorpio
Jul 19	6:00P	Sagittarius
Jul 22	4:00A	Capricorn
Jul 24	5:00P	Aquarius
Jul 27	5:00A	Pisces
Jul 29	5:30P	Aries

June 1983

Jun 2	4:00P	Pisces
Jun 5	3:00A	Aries
Jun 7	11:00A	Taurus
Jun 9	3:45P	Gemini
Jun 11	5:30P	Cancer
Jun 13	6:00P	Leo
Jun 15	7:30P	Virgo
Jun 17	10:30P	Libra
Jun 20	4:00A	Scorpio
Jun 22	12:00P	Sagittarius
Jun 24	10:00P	Capricorn
Jun 27	10:00A	Aquarius
Jun 29	11:00P	Pisces

August 1983

Aug 1	3:45A	Taurus
Aug 3	11:00A	Gemini
Aug 5	2:00P	Cancer
Aug 7	2:30P	Leo
Aug 9	2:00P	Virgo
Aug 11	2:00P	Libra
Aug 13	5:00P	Scorpio
Aug 16	12:00A	Sagittarius
Aug 18	10:00A	Capricorn
Aug 20	10:00P	Aquarius
Aug 23	11:00A	Pisces
Aug 25	11:00P	Aries
Aug 28	10:00A	Taurus
Aug 30	6:00P	Gemini

September 1983

Sep 1	10:30P	Cancer
Sep 4	1:00A	Leo
Sep 6	12:30A	Virgo
Sep 8	12:00A	Libra
Sep 10	2:00A	Scorpio
Sep 12	7:00A	Sagittarius
Sep 14	4:30P	Capricorn
Sep 17	5:00A	Aquarius
Sep 19	5:30P	Pisces
Sep 22	5:30A	Aries
Sep 24	3:00P	Taurus
Sep 29	5:30A	Cancer

November 1983

Nov 1	6:30P	Libra
Nov 4	9:00P	Sagittarius
Nov 6	1:00A	Scorpio
Nov 8	8:30A	Capricorn
Nov 10	7:15P	Aquarius
Nov 13	7:30A	Pisces
Nov 15	7:30P	Aries
Nov 18	5:00A	Taurus
Nov 20	12:00P	Gemini
Nov 22	4:00P	Cancer
Nov 24	7:30P	Leo
Nov 26	10:00P	Virgo
Nov 29	1:00A	Libra

October 1983

Oct 1	9:00A	Leo
Oct 3	10:00A	Virgo
Oct 5	10:30A	Libra
Oct 7	12:00P	Scorpio
Oct 9	4:00P	Sagittarius
Oct 12	12:30A	Capricorn
Oct 14	12:00P	Aquarius
Oct 17	1:00A	Pisces
Oct 19	12:00P	Aries
Oct 21	9:30P	Taurus
Oct 24	5:00A	Gemini
Oct 26	10:30A	Cancer
Oct 28	3:00P	Leo
Oct 30	5:30P	Virgo

December 1983

Dec 1	4:30A	Scorpio
Dec 3	9:30A	Sagittarius
Dec 5	5:30P	Capricorn
Dec 8	4:00A	Aquarius
Dec 10	4:00P	Pisces
Dec 13	4:30A	Aries
Dec 15	2:00P	Taurus
Dec 17	9:00P	Gemini
Dec 20	1:00A	Cancer
Dec 22	3:00A	Leo
Dec 24	4:00A	Virgo
Dec 26	6:30A	Libra
Dec 28	10:30A	Scorpio
Dec 30	5:00P	Sagittarius

January 1984

Jan 2	1:00ᴀ	Capricorn
Jan 4	11:00ᴀ	Aquarius
Jan 6	11:30ᴘ	Pisces
Jan 9	12:00ᴘ	Aries
Jan 12	12:00ᴀ	Taurus
Jan 14	7:30ᴀ	Gemini
Jan 16	11:45ᴀ	Cancer
Jan 18	1:00ᴘ	Leo
Jan 20	12:00ᴘ	Virgo
Jan 22	1:00ᴘ	Libra
Jan 24	4:00ᴘ	Scorpio
Jan 26	10:00ᴘ	Sagittarius
Jan 29	7:15ᴀ	Capricorn
Jan 31	6:00ᴘ	Aquarius

February 1984

Feb 3	6:30ᴀ	Pisces
Feb 5	7:00ᴘ	Aries
Feb 8	7:00ᴀ	Taurus
Feb 10	4:30ᴘ	Gemini
Feb 12	10:00ᴘ	Cancer
Feb 15	12:00ᴀ	Leo
Feb 16	11:30ᴘ	Virgo
Feb 18	11:00ᴘ	Libra
Feb 21	12:00ᴀ	Scorpio
Feb 23	4:30ᴀ	Sagittarius
Feb 25	1:00ᴘ	Capricorn
Feb 28	12:00ᴀ	Aquarius

March 1984

Mar 1	12:30ᴘ	Pisces
Mar 4	1:00ᴀ	Aries
Mar 6	1:00ᴘ	Taurus
Mar 8	11:30ᴘ	Gemini
Mar 11	6:45ᴀ	Cancer
Mar 13	10:00ᴀ	Leo
Mar 15	11:00ᴀ	Virgo
Mar 17	9:30ᴀ	Libra
Mar 19	9:30ᴀ	Scorpio
Mar 21	1:00ᴘ	Sagittarius
Mar 23	7:30ᴘ	Capricorn
Mar 26	6:00ᴀ	Aquarius
Mar 28	6:45ᴘ	Pisces
Mar 31	7:15ᴀ	Aries

April 1984

Apr 2	7:00ᴘ	Taurus
Apr 5	5:00ᴀ	Gemini
Apr 7	1:00ᴘ	Cancer
Apr 9	6:00ᴘ	Leo
Apr 11	8:00ᴘ	Virgo
Apr 13	8:30ᴘ	Libra
Apr 15	9:00ᴘ	Scorpio
Apr 17	11:00ᴘ	Sagittarius
Apr 20	4:00ᴀ	Capricorn
Apr 22	1:30ᴘ	Aquarius
Apr 25	1:00ᴀ	Pisces
Apr 30	2:30ᴀ	Taurus

May 1984

May 2	12:00P	Gemini
May 4	7:30P	Cancer
May 7	12:30A	Leo
May 9	4:00A	Virgo
May 11	6:00A	Libra
May 13	7:30A	Scorpio
May 15	10:00A	Sagittarius
May 17	3:00P	Capricorn
May 19	11:00P	Aquarius
May 22	10:00A	Pisces
May 24	11:00P	Aquarius
May 27	10:00A	Taurus
May 29	7:30P	Gemini

July 1984

Jul 2	3:30P	Virgo
Jul 4	5:00P	Libra
Jul 6	8:30P	Scorpio
Jul 9	1:00A	Sagittarius
Jul 11	7:30A	Capricorn
Jul 13	4:00P	Aquarius
Jul 16	2:00A	Pisces
Jul 18	2:30P	Aries
Jul 21	3:00P	Taurus
Jul 23	1:00P	Gemini
Jul 25	7:45P	Cancer
Jul 27	10:30P	Leo
Jul 29	11:00P	Virgo

June 1984

Jun 1	2:00A	Cancer
Jun 3	6:00A	Leo
Jun 5	9:30A	Virgo
Jun 7	12:00P	Libra
Jun 9	3:00P	Scorpio
Jun 11	6:30P	Sagittarius
Jun 14	12:00A	Capricorn
Jun 16	7:45A	Aquarius
Jun 18	6:00P	Pisces
Jun 21	7:00A	Aries
Jun 23	7:00P	Taurus
Jun 26	4:00A	Gemini
Jun 28	10:00A	Cancer
Jun 30	1:30P	Leo

August 1984

Aug 1	12:00A	Libra
Aug 3	2:00A	Scorpio
Aug 5	6:30A	Sagittarius
Aug 7	1:00P	Capricorn
Aug 9	10:00P	Aquarius
Aug 11	9:30A	Pisces
Aug 15	10:00A	Aries
Aug 17	10:00A	Taurus
Aug 19	9:30P	Gemini
Aug 22	5:00A	Cancer
Aug 24	9:00A	Leo
Aug 26	9:30A	Virgo
Aug 28	9:00A	Libra
Aug 30	9:30A	Scorpio

🌙

September 1984

Sep 1	12:00P	Sagittarius
Sep 3	7:00P	Capricorn
Sep 6	4:00A	Aquarius
Sep 8	3:30P	Pisces
Sep 11	4:00A	Aries
Sep 13	4:30P	Taurus
Sep 16	4:00A	Gemini
Sep 18	1:00P	Cancer
Sep 20	6:30P	Leo
Sep 22	8:15P	Virgo
Sep 24	7:45P	Libra
Sep 26	7:00P	Scorpio
Sep 28	10:30P	Sagittarius

November 1984

Nov 2	3:00A	Pisces
Nov 4	3:00P	Aries
Nov 7	4:00A	Taurus
Nov 9	3:00P	Gemini
Nov 12	12:30A	Cancer
Nov 14	7:30A	Leo
Nov 16	12:00P	Virgo
Nov 18	2:00P	Libra
Nov 20	3:00P	Scorpio
Nov 22	4:00P	Sagittarius
Nov 24	7:30P	Capricorn
Nov 27	1:00A	Aquarius
Nov 29	11:00A	Pisces

October 1984

Oct 1	1:30A	Capricorn
Oct 3	10:00A	Aquarius
Oct 5	9:30P	Pisces
Oct 8	10:00A	Aries
Oct 10	11:00P	Taurus
Oct 13	10:00A	Gemini
Oct 15	8:00A	Cancer
Oct 18	2:30A	Leo
Oct 20	6:30A	Virgo
Oct 22	6:30A	Libra
Oct 24	6:00A	Scorpio
Oct 26	7:00A	Sagittarius
Oct 28	10:00A	Capricorn
Oct 30	4:00P	Aquarius

December 1984

Dec 1	11:00P	Aries
Dec 4	11:00A	Taurus
Dec 6	10:30P	Gemini
Dec 9	7:00P	Cancer
Dec 11	1:00P	Leo
Dec 13	5:30P	Virgo
Dec 15	9:00P	Libra
Dec 17	11:30P	Scorpio
Dec 20	2:00A	Sagittarius
Dec 22	5:30A	Capricorn
Dec 24	11:00A	Aquarius
Dec 26	7:30P	Pisces
Dec 29	6:50A	Aries

MOON CHARTS
(EST & EDT)

☾

January 1985

Jan 1	7:30P	Taurus
Jan 3	7:00P	Gemini
Jan 5	3:00P	Cancer
Jan 7	8:30P	Leo
Jan 10	12:00A	Virgo
Jan 12	12:00A	Libra
Jan 14	5:00A	Scorpio
Jan 16	9:00A	Sagittarius
Jan 18	1:15P	Capricorn
Jan 20	7:30P	Aquarius
Jan 23	4:00A	Pisces
Jan 25	3:00P	Aries
Jan 28	4:00A	Taurus
Jan 30	4:00P	Gemini

February 1985

Feb 2	1:00A	Cancer
Feb 4	6:00A	Leo
Feb 6	8:00A	Virgo
Feb 8	9:00A	Libra
Feb 10	11:00A	Scorpio
Feb 12	2:00P	Sagittarius
Feb 14	7:30P	Capricorn
Feb 17	3:00A	Aquarius
Feb 19	12:00P	Pisces
Feb 21	11:00P	Aries
Feb 24	11:30A	Taurus
Feb 27	12:30A	Gemini

March 1985

Mar 1	10:30A	Cancer
Mar 3	4:00P	Leo
Mar 5	6:45P	Virgo
Mar 7	6:50P	Libra
Mar 9	6:50P	Scorpio
Mar 11	8:30P	Sagittarius
Mar 14	1:00A	Capricorn
Mar 16	8:00A	Aquarius
Mar 18	6:00P	Pisces
Mar 21	5:30A	Aries
Mar 23	6:00P	Taurus
Mar 26	7:00P	Gemini
Mar 28	6:00P	Cancer
Mar 31	2:00A	Leo

April 1985

Apr 2	5:30A	Virgo
Apr 4	5:30A	Libra
Apr 6	5:00A	Scorpio
Apr 8	5:00A	Sagittarius
Apr 10	8:00A	Capricorn
Apr 12	2:00P	Aquarius
Apr 14	11:00P	Pisces
Apr 17	11:00A	Aries
Apr 20	12:30A	Taurus
Apr 22	1:00A	Gemini
Apr 25	12:30A	Cancer
Apr 27	9:00A	Leo
Apr 29	3:00P	Virgo

MOON CHARTS
(EST & EDT)

May 1985

May 1	5:00P	Libra
May 3	5:00P	Scorpio
May 5	5:00P	Sagittarius
May 7	6:00P	Capricorn
May 9	10:15P	Aquarius
May 12	7:00A	Pisces
May 14	6:30P	Aries
May 17	7:30A	Taurus
May 19	8:00A	Gemini
May 22	7:00A	Cancer
May 24	4:00P	Leo
May 26	10:00P	Virgo
May 29	2:00A	Libra
May 31	2:30A	Scorpio

June 1985

Jun 2	3:00A	Sagittarius
Jun 4	4:15A	Capricorn
Jun 6	8:00A	Aquarius
Jun 8	3:00P	Pisces
Jun 11	1:30A	Aries
Jun 13	2:00P	Taurus
Jun 16	3:00P	Gemini
Jun 18	1:45P	Cancer
Jun 20	9:30P	Leo
Jun 23	3:00A	Virgo
Jun 25	7:45A	Libra
Jun 27	10:00P	Scorpio
Jun 29	12:00P	Sagittarius

July 1985

Jul 1	2:30P	Capricorn
Jul 3	6:00P	Aquarius
Jul 6	12:00A	Pisces
Jul 8	9:30A	Aries
Jul 10	10:00P	Taurus
Jul 12	9:40P	Gemini
Jul 15	10:00P	Cancer
Jul 18	4:00A	Leo
Jul 20	9:30A	Virgo
Jul 22	1:00P	Libra
Jul 24	4:00P	Scorpio
Jul 26	7:00P	Sagittarius
Jul 28	10:30P	Capricorn
Jul 31	2:00A	Aquarius

August 1985

Aug 2	8:30A	Pisces
Aug 4	6:00P	Aries
Aug 7	5:45A	Taurus
Aug 9	6:30P	Gemini
Aug 12	5:30A	Cancer
Aug 14	1:00P	Leo
Aug 16	5:30P	Virgo
Aug 18	7:45P	Libra
Aug 20	9:30P	Scorpio
Aug 23	12:15A	Sagittarius
Aug 25	4:00A	Capricorn
Aug 27	10:00A	Aquarius
Aug 29	4:00P	Pisces

September 1985

Sep 1	2:00A	Aries
Sep 3	1:30P	Taurus
Sep 6	2:30A	Gemini
Sep 8	2:00P	Cancer
Sep 10	8:00P	Leo
Sep 13	3:00A	Virgo
Sep 15	4:00A	Libra
Sep 17	5:30A	Scorpio
Sep 19	7:00A	Sagittarius
Sep 21	10:00A	Capricorn
Sep 23	3:00P	Aquarius
Sep 25	11:00P	Pisces
Sep 28	7:45A	Aries
Sep 30	8:30P	Taurus

November 1985

Nov 2	3:30A	Cancer
Nov 4	2:00P	Leo
Nov 6	9:00P	Virgo
Nov 9	1:00A	Libra
Nov 11	1:30A	Scorpio
Nov 13	1:00A	Sagittarius
Nov 15	1:00A	Capricorn
Nov 17	3:15A	Aquarius
Nov 19	10:00A	Pisces
Nov 21	8:00P	Aries
Nov 24	8:00A	Taurus
Nov 26	9:00P	Gemini
Nov 29	9:00A	Cancer

October 1985

Oct 3	9:30A	Gemini
Oct 5	10:00P	Cancer
Oct 8	7:30A	Leo
Oct 10	1:00P	Virgo
Oct 12	2:30P	Libra
Oct 14	2:30P	Scorpio
Oct 16	2:30P	Sagittarius
Oct 18	4:15P	Capricorn
Oct 20	9:00P	Aquarius
Oct 23	4:30A	Pisces
Oct 25	3:00P	Aries
Oct 28	2:00A	Taurus
Oct 30	3:00P	Gemini

December 1985

Dec 1	8:00P	Leo
Dec 4	4:00A	Virgo
Dec 6	10:00A	Libra
Dec 8	12:00P	Scorpio
Dec 10	12:50P	Sagittarius
Dec 12	12:45P	Capricorn
Dec 14	1:30P	Aquarius
Dec 16	6:00P	Pisces
Dec 19	2:45A	Aries
Dec 21	3:00P	Taurus
Dec 24	4:00A	Gemini
Dec 26	4:00P	Cancer
Dec 29	4:00A	Leo
Dec 31	9:30A	Virgo

MOON CHARTS
(EST & EDT)
☽

January 1986

Jan 2	3:30P	Libra
Jan 4	7:30P	Scorpio
Jan 6	9:30P	Sagittarius
Jan 8	10:00P	Capricorn
Jan 11	12:00A	Aquarius
Jan 13	3:45A	Pisces
Jan 15	11:00A	Aries
Jan 17	10:30P	Taurus
Jan 20	11:00A	Gemini
Jan 22	11:00P	Cancer
Jan 25	9:00A	Leo
Jan 27	3:45P	Virgo
Jan 29	9:00P	Libra

February 1986

Feb 1	1:00A	Scorpio
Feb 3	4:00A	Sagittarius
Feb 5	7:00P	Capricorn
Feb 7	10:00A	Aquarius
Feb 9	1:30P	Pisces
Feb 11	8:30P	Aries
Feb 14	7:45A	Taurus
Feb 16	7:30P	Gemini
Feb 19	7:30P	Cancer
Feb 21	5:30P	Leo
Feb 24	12:30A	Virgo
Feb 26	4:00A	Libra
Feb 28	7:10A	Scorpio

March 1986

Mar 2	10:00A	Sagittarius
Mar 4	1:00P	Capricorn
Mar 6	4:45P	Aquarius
Mar 8	10:00P	Pisces
Mar 11	5:00A	Aries
Mar 13	3:00P	Taurus
Mar 16	3:45A	Gemini
Mar 18	4:00P	Cancer
Mar 21	3:00A	Leo
Mar 23	10:00A	Virgo
Mar 25	1:00P	Libra
Mar 27	3:00P	Scorpio
Mar 29	4:00P	Sagittarius
Mar 31	6:30P	Capricorn

April 1986

Apr 2	10:00P	Aquarius
Apr 5	4:00A	Pisces
Apr 7	1:30P	Aries
Apr 10	12:00A	Taurus
Apr 12	12:00P	Gemini
Apr 15	1:00A	Cancer
Apr 17	12:00P	Leo
Apr 19	8:30P	Virgo
Apr 22	12:30A	Libra
Apr 24	2:00A	Scorpio
Apr 26	2:00P	Sagittarius
Apr 28	3:00A	Capricorn
Apr 30	5:00A	Aquarius

MOON CHARTS
(EST & EDT)

May 1986

May 2	8:30A	Pisces
May 4	7:00P	Aries
May 7	6:00A	Taurus
May 9	6:30P	Gemini
May 12	7:20A	Cancer
May 14	7:15P	Leo
May 17	5:00A	Virgo
May 19	10:30A	Libra
May 21	1:00P	Scorpio
May 23	1:00P	Sagittarius
May 25	12:00P	Capricorn
May 27	1:00P	Aquarius
May 29	5:00P	Pisces

June 1986

Jun 1	12:45A	Aries
Jun 3	12:00P	Taurus
Jun 6	12:00A	Gemini
Jun 8	1:30P	Cancer
Jun 11	1:30A	Leo
Jun 13	11:00A	Virgo
Jun 15	6:30P	Libra
Jun 17	10:30P	Scorpio
Jun 19	11:00P	Sagittarius
Jun 21	11:00P	Capricorn
Jun 23	11:00P	Aquarius
Jun 26	1:00A	Pisces
Jun 28	7:30A	Aries
Jun 30	5:00P	Taurus

July 1986

Jul 3	6:30A	Gemini
Jul 5	7:30P	Cancer
Jul 8	7:00A	Leo
Jul 10	4:45P	Virgo
Jul 13	12:15A	Libra
Jul 15	6:00P	Scorpio
Jul 17	8:30A	Sagittarius
Jul 19	9:00A	Capricorn
Jul 21	9:30A	Aquarius
Jul 23	11:00A	Pisces
Jul 25	4:00P	Aries
Jul 28	1:30A	Taurus
Jul 30	1:30P	Gemini

August 1986

Aug 2	2:00P	Cancer
Aug 4	1:30P	Leo
Aug 6	10:30P	Virgo
Aug 9	6:00A	Libra
Aug 11	11:00A	Scorpio
Aug 13	3:00P	Sagittarius
Aug 15	5:00P	Capricorn
Aug 17	7:00P	Aquarius
Aug 19	9:00P	Pisces
Aug 22	1:30A	Aries
Aug 24	9:30A	Taurus
Aug 26	9:00P	Gemini
Aug 29	10:00A	Cancer
Aug 31	9:00P	Leo

September 1986

Sep 3	6:00A	Virgo
Sep 5	12:30P	Libra
Sep 7	5:00P	Scorpio
Sep 9	8:30P	Sagittarius
Sep 11	11:30P	Capricorn
Sep 14	2:00A	Aquarius
Sep 16	5:00A	Pisces
Sep 18	10:30A	Aries
Sep 20	6:30P	Taurus
Sep 23	5:30A	Gemini
Sep 25	5:45P	Cancer
Sep 28	5:45A	Leo
Sep 30	3:00P	Virgo

November 1986

Nov 1	9:00A	Scorpio
Nov 3	10:00A	Sagittarius
Nov 5	10:30A	Capricorn
Nov 7	12:00P	Aquarius
Nov 9	4:00P	Pisces
Nov 11	11:00P	Aries
Nov 14	8:30A	Taurus
Nov 16	7:30P	Gemini
Nov 19	8:00A	Cancer
Nov 21	8:00P	Leo
Nov 24	8:00A	Virgo
Nov 26	4:00P	Libra
Nov 28	8:00P	Scorpio
Nov 30	9:00P	Sagittarius

October 1986

Oct 2	9:00P	Libra
Oct 5	1:00A	Scorpio
Oct 7	3:00A	Sagittarius
Oct 9	5:00A	Capricorn
Oct 11	7:50A	Aquarius
Oct 13	12:00P	Pisces
Oct 15	6:00P	Aries
Oct 18	3:00A	Taurus
Oct 20	1:00P	Gemini
Oct 23	2:00A	Cancer
Oct 25	2:00P	Leo
Oct 28	12:00A	Virgo
Oct 30	7:00A	Libra

December 1986

Dec 2	8:30P	Capricorn
Dec 4	8:30P	Aquarius
Dec 6	11:00P	Pisces
Dec 9	5:00A	Aries
Dec 11	2:00P	Taurus
Dec 14	2:00A	Gemini
Dec 16	2:00P	Cancer
Dec 19	3:00A	Leo
Dec 21	3:00P	Virgo
Dec 24	12:00A	Libra
Dec 26	6:00A	Scorpio
Dec 28	8:00A	Sagittarius
Dec 30	8:00A	Capricorn

January 1987

Jan 1	7:00P	Aquarius
Jan 3	7:30P	Pisces
Jan 5	12:00P	Aries
Jan 7	8:00P	Taurus
Jan 10	7:30P	Gemini
Jan 12	8:00P	Cancer
Jan 15	9:00A	Leo
Jan 17	8:00P	Virgo
Jan 20	6:00A	Libra
Jan 22	1:00P	Scorpio
Jan 24	5:30P	Sagittarius
Jan 26	6:45P	Capricorn
Jan 28	6:15P	Aquarius
Jan 30	6:30P	Pisces

March 1987

Mar 1	7:30A	Aries
Mar 3	1:00P	Taurus
Mar 5	10:30P	Gemini
Mar 8	10:30A	Cancer
Mar 10	11:00P	Leo
Mar 13	10:00A	Virgo
Mar 15	6:30P	Libra
Mar 18	12:45A	Scorpio
Mar 20	5:30A	Sagittarius
Mar 22	9:00A	Capricorn
Mar 24	11:00A	Aquarius
Mar 26	2:00P	Pisces
Mar 28	5:00P	Aries
Mar 30	11:00P	Taurus

February 1987

Feb 1	9:00P	Aries
Feb 4	4:00A	Taurus
Feb 6	2:15P	Gemini
Feb 9	3:00A	Cancer
Feb 11	3:30P	Leo
Feb 14	2:00P	Virgo
Feb 16	12:00P	Libra
Feb 18	7:00P	Scorpio
Feb 21	12:00A	Sagittarius
Feb 23	2:30A	Capricorn
Feb 25	4:00A	Aquarius
Feb 27	5:00P	Pisces

April 1987

Apr 2	7:30A	Gemini
Apr 4	6:30P	Cancer
Apr 7	8:00A	Leo
Apr 9	7:30P	Virgo
Apr 12	4:00A	Libra
Apr 14	10:00A	Scorpio
Apr 16	1:00P	Sagittarius
Apr 18	3:00P	Capricorn
Apr 20	6:00P	Aquarius
Apr 22	9:00P	Pisces
Apr 25	2:00A	Aries
Apr 27	8:00A	Taurus
Apr 29	5:00P	Gemini

May 1987

May 2	4:00A	Cancer
May 4	4:30P	Leo
May 7	4:00A	Virgo
May 9	1:00P	Libra
May 11	7:00P	Scorpio
May 13	10:00P	Sagittarius
May 15	10:30P	Capricorn
May 18	12:00A	Aquarius
May 20	2:15A	Pisces
May 22	7:30A	Aries
May 24	3:00P	Taurus
May 27	12:00A	Gemini
May 29	11:00A	Cancer
May 31	11:45P	Leo

July 1987

Jul 3	6:00A	Libra
Jul 5	2:00P	Scorpio
Jul 7	6:00P	Sagittarius
Jul 9	6:45P	Capricorn
Jul 11	6:00P	Aquarius
Jul 13	6:00P	Pisces
Jul 15	8:00P	Aries
Jul 18	2:00A	Taurus
Jul 20	12:00P	Gemini
Jul 22	11:00P	Cancer
Jul 25	12:00P	Leo
Jul 28	12:30A	Virgo
Jul 30	12:00P	Libra

June 1987

Jun 3	12:00A	Virgo
Jun 6	10:00A	Libra
Jun 8	5:00A	Scorpio
Jun 10	8:00A	Sagittarius
Jun 12	8:00A	Capricorn
Jun 14	8:00A	Aquarius
Jun 16	9:00A	Pisces
Jun 18	1:00P	Aries
Jun 20	8:00P	Taurus
Jun 23	6:00A	Gemini
Jun 25	5:00P	Cancer
Jun 28	6:00A	Leo
Jun 30	6:30P	Virgo

August 1987

Aug 1	9:00P	Scorpio
Aug 4	3:00A	Sagittarius
Aug 6	5:00A	Capricorn
Aug 8	5:00A	Aquarius
Aug 10	4:00A	Pisces
Aug 12	5:00A	Aries
Aug 14	10:00A	Taurus
Aug 16	6:00P	Gemini
Aug 19	5:00A	Cancer
Aug 21	6:00P	Leo
Aug 24	6:30A	Virgo
Aug 26	5:45P	Libra
Aug 29	3:00A	Scorpio
Aug 31	9:30A	Sagittarius

September 1987

Sep 2	1:00P	Capricorn
Sep 4	2:00P	Aquarius
Sep 6	2:30P	Pisces
Sep 8	4:00P	Aries
Sep 10	7:00P	Taurus
Sep 13	2:00A	Gemini
Sep 15	1:00P	Cancer
Sep 18	1:00A	Leo
Sep 20	1:00P	Virgo
Sep 23	12:00A	Libra
Sep 25	8:30A	Scorpio
Sep 27	3:00P	Sagittarius
Sep 29	7:00P	Capricorn

November 1987

Nov 2	9:00A	Aries
Nov 4	1:00P	Taurus
Nov 6	7:15P	Gemini
Nov 9	4:00A	Cancer
Nov 11	4:00P	Leo
Nov 14	4:30A	Virgo
Nov 16	3:45P	Libra
Nov 18	11:30P	Scorpio
Nov 21	4:00A	Sagittarius
Nov 23	6:30P	Capricorn
Nov 25	8:30A	Aquarius
Nov 27	10:30A	Pisces
Nov 29	2:30P	Aries

October 1987

Oct 3	10:00A	Aquarius
Oct 4	12:00A	Pisces
Oct 6	1:00A	Aries
Oct 8	5:00A	Taurus
Oct 10	11:00A	Gemini
Oct 12	8:30P	Cancer
Oct 15	8:30A	Leo
Oct 17	9:00P	Virgo
Oct 20	7:45A	Libra
Oct 22	3:30P	Scorpio
Oct 24	9:00P	Sagittarius
Oct 26	11:00P	Capricorn
Oct 29	2:30A	Aquarius
Oct 31	5:00A	Pisces

December 1987

Dec 1	8:00P	Taurus
Dec 4	3:00A	Gemini
Dec 6	12:00P	Cancer
Dec 9	12:00A	Leo
Dec 11	12:45P	Virgo
Dec 14	12:30A	Libra
Dec 16	9:00A	Scorpio
Dec 18	2:00P	Sagittarius
Dec 20	4:00P	Capricorn
Dec 22	4:00P	Aquarius
Dec 24	5:00P	Pisces
Dec 26	8:00P	Aries
Dec 29	1:15A	Taurus
Dec 31	9:30A	Gemini

January 1988		
Jan 2	7:15P	Cancer
Jan 5	6:45A	Leo
Jan 7	7:30P	Virgo
Jan 10	8:00A	Libra
Jan 12	6:30P	Scorpio
Jan 15	1:00A	Sagittarius
Jan 17	3:00A	Capricorn
Jan 19	3:00A	Aquarius
Jan 21	2:00A	Pisces
Jan 23	3:15A	Aries
Jan 25	7:30P	Taurus
Jan 27	3:00P	Gemini
Jan 30	1:00A	Cancer

March 1988		
Mar 2	8:00A	Virgo
Mar 4	8:30P	Libra
Mar 7	7:30P	Scorpio
Mar 9	4:00P	Sagittarius
Mar 11	9:30P	Capricorn
Mar 13	11:30P	Aquarius
Mar 16	12:30A	Pisces
Mar 18	1:00A	Aries
Mar 20	2:00A	Taurus
Mar 22	6:30A	Gemini
Mar 24	2:30P	Cancer
Mar 27	2:00A	Leo
Mar 29	3:00P	Virgo

February 1988		
Feb 1	1:00A	Leo
Feb 4	2:00A	Virgo
Feb 6	2:45P	Libra
Feb 9	1:30A	Scorpio
Feb 11	9:15A	Sagittarius
Feb 13	1:30P	Capricorn
Feb 15	1:45P	Aquarius
Feb 17	1:30P	Pisces
Feb 19	2:00P	Aries
Feb 21	4:00P	Taurus
Feb 23	9:30P	Gemini
Feb 26	7:15A	Cancer
Feb 28	7:15P	Leo

April 1988		
Apr 1	3:00A	Libra
Apr 3	2:00P	Scorpio
Apr 5	10:30P	Sagittarius
Apr 8	4:00A	Capricorn
Apr 10	8:15A	Aquarius
Apr 12	10:00A	Capricorn
Apr 14	11:15P	Aries
Apr 16	1:00P	Taurus
Apr 18	5:00P	Gemini
Apr 21	12:00A	Cancer
Apr 23	11:00A	Leo
Apr 25	11:30P	Virgo
Apr 28	11:00A	Libra
Apr 30	9:30P	Scorpio

MOON CHARTS
(EST & EDT)
☾

May 1988

May 3	5:00A	Sagittarius
May 5	10:00A	Capricorn
May 7	1:30P	Aquarius
May 9	4:00P	Pisces
May 11	7:30P	Aries
May 13	10:00P	Taurus
May 16	2:00A	Gemini
May 18	9:15A	Cancer
May 20	7:00P	Leo
May 23	7:00A	Virgo
May 25	7:50A	Libra
May 28	6:00A	Scorpio
May 30	12:30P	Sagittarius

June 1988

Jun 1	5:00P	Capricorn
Jun 3	7:30P	Aquarius
Jun 5	10:00P	Pisces
Jun 8	12:30A	Aries
Jun 10	5:00A	Taurus
Jun 12	10:00A	Gemini
Jun 14	5:30P	Cancer
Jun 17	3:00A	Leo
Jun 19	3:00P	Virgo
Jun 22	4:00A	Libra
Jun 24	3:00P	Scorpio
Jun 26	10:00P	Sagittarius
Jun 29	2:00A	Capricorn

July 1988

Jul 1	3:15A	Aquarius
Jul 3	4:15A	Pisces
Jul 5	6:30A	Aries
Jul 7	10:30A	Taurus
Jul 9	4:00P	Gemini
Jul 12	12:00A	Cancer
Jul 14	10:00A	Leo
Jul 16	10:30P	Virgo
Jul 19	11:30A	Libra
Jul 21	11:00P	Scorpio
Jul 24	7:45A	Sagittarius
Jul 26	12:00P	Capricorn
Jul 28	1:00P	Aquarius
Jul 30	1:00P	Pisces

August 1988

Aug 1	1:30P	Aries
Aug 3	4:00P	Taurus
Aug 5	10:00P	Gemini
Aug 8	5:00A	Cancer
Aug 10	4:30P	Leo
Aug 13	5:00A	Virgo
Aug 15	6:00P	Libra
Aug 18	6:00A	Scorpio
Aug 20	4:00P	Sagittarius
Aug 22	10:00P	Capricorn
Aug 25	12:00A	Aquarius
Aug 27	12:00A	Pisces
Aug 28	11:30P	Aries
Aug 31	12:30A	Taurus

September 1988

Sep 2	4:00A	Gemini
Sep 4	11:45A	Cancer
Sep 6	10:00P	Leo
Sep 9	11:00A	Virgo
Sep 12	12:00A	Libra
Sep 14	12:00P	Scorpio
Sep 16	10:15P	Sagittarius
Sep 19	5:45A	Capricorn
Sep 21	10:00A	Aquarius
Sep 23	10:30A	Pisces
Sep 25	10:30A	Aries
Sep 27	10:30A	Taurus
Sep 29	12:30P	Gemini

November 1988

Nov 3	11:00A	Virgo
Nov 5	12:00P	Libra
Nov 8	12:00A	Scorpio
Nov 10	9:00A	Sagittarius
Nov 12	4:00P	Capricorn
Nov 14	9:30P	Aquarius
Nov 17	1:30A	Pisces
Nov 19	4:00A	Aries
Nov 21	6:00A	Taurus
Nov 23	8:30A	Gemini
Nov 25	12:30P	Cancer
Nov 27	8:00P	Leo
Nov 30	7:00A	Virgo

October 1988

Oct 1	6:30P	Cancer
Oct 4	4:30A	Leo
Oct 6	5:00P	Virgo
Oct 9	6:00A	Libra
Oct 11	6:00P	Scorpio
Oct 14	4:00A	Sagittarius
Oct 16	12:00P	Capricorn
Oct 18	5:00P	Aquarius
Oct 20	8:00P	Pisces
Oct 22	9:00P	Aries
Oct 24	9:30P	Taurus
Oct 26	10:30P	Gemini
Oct 29	3:30A	Cancer
Oct 31	11:00A	Leo

December 1988

Dec 2	8:00P	Libra
Dec 5	8:00A	Scorpio
Dec 7	5:00P	Sagittarius
Dec 10	11:00A	Capricorn
Dec 12	3:15A	Aquarius
Dec 14	7:00A	Pisces
Dec 16	9:30A	Aries
Dec 18	1:15A	Taurus
Dec 20	4:45P	Gemini
Dec 22	9:30P	Cancer
Dec 25	5:00A	Leo
Dec 27	3:45P	Virgo
Dec 30	4:15A	Libra

January 1989

Jan 1	4:45P	Scorpio
Jan 4	2:00A	Sagittarius
Jan 6	8:00A	Capricorn
Jan 8	11:30A	Aquarius
Jan 10	1:30P	Pisces
Jan 12	3:00P	Aries
Jan 14	6:45P	Taurus
Jan 16	11:00P	Gemini
Jan 19	5:00A	Cancer
Jan 21	1:00P	Leo
Jan 24	12:00A	Virgo
Jan 26	12:00P	Libra
Jan 29	1:00A	Scorpio
Jan 31	11:30A	Sagittarius

February 1989

Feb 2	6:30P	Capricorn
Feb 4	10:00P	Aquarius
Feb 6	10:30P	Pisces
Feb 8	10:40P	Aries
Feb 11	12:45A	Taurus
Feb 13	4:00A	Gemini
Feb 15	10:45A	Cancer
Feb 17	7:30P	Leo
Feb 20	6:30A	Virgo
Feb 22	7:10P	Libra
Feb 25	8:00A	Scorpio
Feb 27	7:30P	Sagittarius

March 1989

Mar 2	4:00P	Capricorn
Mar 4	8:30A	Aquarius
Mar 6	10:00A	Pisces
Mar 8	9:30A	Aries
Mar 10	9:30A	Taurus
Mar 12	11:30A	Gemini
Mar 14	4:00P	Cancer
Mar 17	1:30A	Leo
Mar 19	12:45P	Virgo
Mar 22	1:00A	Libra
Mar 24	2:00P	Scorpio
Mar 27	2:00A	Sagittarius
Mar 29	11:00A	Capricorn
Mar 31	6:00P	Aquarius

April 1989

Apr 2	9:45P	Pisces
Apr 4	9:45P	Aries
Apr 6	9:00P	Taurus
Apr 8	9:30P	Gemini
Apr 11	1:00A	Cancer
Apr 13	8:30A	Leo
Apr 15	7:45P	Virgo
Apr 18	8:30A	Libra
Apr 20	9:00P	Scorpio
Apr 23	8:30A	Sagittarius
Apr 25	6:30P	Capricorn
Apr 28	1:00A	Aquarius
Apr 30	6:00A	Pisces

MOON CHARTS
(EST & EDT)
🌙

May 1989

May 2	7:50A	Aries
May 4	8:00A	Taurus
May 6	8:00A	Gemini
May 8	10:00A	Cancer
May 10	4:30P	Leo
May 13	2:30A	Virgo
May 15	3:00P	Libra
May 18	4:00A	Scorpio
May 20	3:00P	Sagittarius
May 23	12:00A	Capricorn
May 25	7:00A	Aquarius
May 27	12:15P	Pisces
May 29	3:00P	Aries
May 31	5:00P	Taurus

July 1989

Jul 2	5:00A	Cancer
Jul 4	10:30A	Leo
Jul 6	7:00P	Virgo
Jul 9	6:30A	Libra
Jul 11	7:15P	Scorpio
Jul 14	6:30A	Sagittarius
Jul 16	3:00P	Capricorn
Jul 18	8:30P	Aquarius
Jul 21	12:15A	Pisces
Jul 23	2:30A	Aries
Jul 25	5:00A	Taurus
Jul 27	8:30A	Gemini
Jul 29	12:30P	Cancer
Jul 31	7:00P	Leo

June 1989

Jun 2	6:00P	Gemini
Jun 4	8:30P	Cancer
Jun 7	1:30A	Leo
Jun 9	10:30A	Virgo
Jun 11	11:00P	Libra
Jun 14	11:30A	Scorpio
Jun 16	10:30P	Sagittarius
Jun 19	6:45A	Capricorn
Jun 21	1:00P	Aquarius
Jun 23	5:30P	Pisces
Jun 25	9:00P	Aries
Jun 28	12:00A	Taurus
Jun 30	2:00A	Gemini

August 1989

Aug 3	3:30A	Virgo
Aug 5	2:30P	Libra
Aug 8	3:00A	Scorpio
Aug 10	3:00P	Sagittarius
Aug 13	12:00A	Capricorn
Aug 15	6:00A	Aquarius
Aug 17	9:00A	Pisces
Aug 19	10:00A	Aries
Aug 21	11:30A	Taurus
Aug 23	1:30P	Gemini
Aug 25	6:00P	Cancer
Aug 28	1:00A	Leo
Aug 30	10:00A	Virgo

MOON CHARTS
(EST & EDT)

🌙

September 1989

Sep 1	10:00P	Libra
Sep 4	10:00A	Scorpio
Sep 6	11:00P	Sagittarius
Sep 9	9:00A	Capricorn
Sep 11	4:00P	Aquarius
Sep 13	7:00P	Pisces
Sep 15	7:30P	Aries
Sep 17	7:30P	Taurus
Sep 19	8:30P	Gemini
Sep 22	12:00A	Cancer
Sep 24	7:00A	Leo
Sep 26	4:45P	Virgo
Sep 29	4:30A	Libra

November 1989

Nov 2	10:00P	Capricorn
Nov 5	7:00A	Aquarius
Nov 7	1:15P	Pisces
Nov 9	4:00P	Aries
Nov 11	4:00P	Taurus
Nov 13	3:00P	Gemini
Nov 15	4:00P	Cancer
Nov 17	7:45P	Leo
Nov 20	4:00A	Virgo
Nov 22	3:45P	Libra
Nov 25	4:00A	Scorpio
Nov 27	4:30P	Sagittarius
Nov 30	3:30A	Capricorn

October 1989

Oct 1	5:00P	Scorpio
Oct 4	5:45A	Sagittarius
Oct 6	5:00P	Capricorn
Oct 9	12:30A	Aquarius
Oct 11	5:15A	Pisces
Oct 13	6:30A	Aries
Oct 15	5:30A	Taurus
Oct 17	5:00A	Gemini
Oct 19	7:00A	Cancer
Oct 21	1:00P	Leo
Oct 23	10:00P	Virgo
Oct 26	10:00A	Libra
Oct 28	10:00P	Scorpio
Oct 31	10:00A	Sagittarius

December 1989

Dec 2	12:30P	Aquarius
Dec 4	8:00P	Pisces
Dec 6	11:40P	Aries
Dec 9	1:30A	Taurus
Dec 11	1:40A	Gemini
Dec 13	2:30A	Cancer
Dec 15	6:00A	Leo
Dec 17	12:30P	Virgo
Dec 19	11:00P	Libra
Dec 21	10:30P	Scorpio
Dec 24	11:00P	Sagittarius
Dec 27	10:30A	Capricorn
Dec 29	6:30P	Aquarius

THANK YOU, THANK YOU . . .

I had a great time writing this book, and I appreciate all the people who made it possible. At Warner Books: special thanks to Jackie Joiner for her editorial expertise, and to Jamie Raab, Les Pockell, Jean Griffin, and Stacy Ashton for their support of this book! Kisses to my literary agents, Lisa Hagan and Sandra Martin, for their unwavering belief in me and my work. High fives to my friends for putting up with my phone calls at all hours in search of their advice, wisdom, and laughter: Michelle Amlong, Maureen Jeffries, Lynne McCann-Delgado, and Breena Alongi. A hug to my astrologically astute sweetheart, Ed Lamadrid. And last but not least, to my parents, Harvey and Roberta Wolf: Thank you!

ABOUT THE AUTHOR

STACEY WOLF is a professional psychic and spiritual counselor in New York City. She has appeared on numerous TV and radio shows throughout the country, including *The View* and *The Roseanne Show*. Stacey is the author of *Stacey Wolf's Psychic Living: A Complete Guide to Enhancing Your Life with Universal Energy* and is featured in *The 100 Top Psychics in America*.